Caste : its supposed origin: its history; its effects : the duty of government, Hindus, and Christians with respect to it; and its prospects

John Murdoch

PAPERS ON INDIAN REFORM.

CASTE:

ITS SUPPOSED ORIGIN; ITS HISTORY; ITS EFFECTS; THE DUTY OF GOVERNMENT, HINDUS, AND CHRISTIANS WITH RESPECT TO IT, AND ITS PROSPECTS.

THIRD EDITION, 3,000—TOTAL COPIES, 9,000

"The longer one lives, observes, and thinks, the more deeply does he feel there is no community on the face of the earth which suffers less from political evils and more from self-inflicted, or self-accepted, or self-created, and, therefore, avoidable evils, than the Hindu community!!"

Raja Sir T. Madhava Row, K C S I.

Caste —**" The most disastrous and blighting of human institutions "**

" Ancient Law " by *Sir H. S. Maine.*

"One of the constant duties of a loyal citizen will be to help to bring back the golden day of the Krita-Yuga, by breaking down the walls of partition that sever brothers from brothers."

Rev. E. P. Rice, B A.

THE CHRISTIAN LITERATURE SOCIETY FOR INDIA
LONDON AND MADRAS
1896.

PREFATORY NOTE.

Caste has been well described as "the most intolerant and exacting taskmaster that ever placed a yoke on the neck of man." It is a pleasing sign of progress that its evils are beginning to be felt, and that some intelligent Indians are seeking to deliver their country from its bondage The present pamphlet is intended to aid these reformers in their noble design Many have not access to Public Libraries, and it is expensive to purchase all the books that require to be examined. The compiler has sought to bring together, within moderate compass, the opinions of some of the best Oriental scholars, Indian and European, bearing on the subject. The following are the works which have chiefly been consulted .—

Asiatic Quarterly Review
Banerjea, Rev. Dr. Krishna Mohun, *Essay on Caste.*
Barth, *Religions of India*
Bhattacharyya, K. K., *Tagore Law Lectures.*
Bower, Rev Dr H. *Prize Essay on Hindu Caste*
Cotton, H. J S, *New India.*
Dubois, *Manners and Customs of the People of India.*
Duff, Rev Dr, *The Indian Rebellion*
Hunter, Sir W. W, *India*
Madras Census Reports for 1871 and 1881
Manu's Ordinances, translated by Burnell.
Mitchell, Rev. Dr Murray, *Hinduism Past and Present.*
Muir, Dr. John, *Sanskrit Texts.*
Müller, Professor Max, Works.
Sherring, Rev. M A., *Hindu Tribes and Castes.*
Siromani, J. S., *Commentary on Hindu Law.*
Wilkins, W. J., *Modern Hinduism.*
Williams, Sir Monier, *Religious Thought and Life in India.*
Wilson, Rev. Dr, *Indian Caste*

Some of the leading Native newspapers have also furnished materials.

National vanity and false patriotism may be unwilling to listen to anything from a foreigner. Some Indian critics, instead of directing attention to the subject, may simply follow the well-known legal advice, "Abuse plaintiff's attorney." On the other hand, the Romans, the greatest conquerors of antiquity, held the maxim, *Fas est ab hoste doceri,* It is allowable to learn even from an enemy. But the compiler expects more generous treatment from others.

If a darker view has been taken of caste than is usually entertained, it is substantially that expressed by some of the ablest men who have studied the subject. Readers, however, should use their own judgment, and draw their own conclusions.

MADRAS, *September,* 1887. J. MURDOCH.

CONTENTS.

CASTE.

INTRODUCTION.

The English word *Caste* is probably derived from the Portuguese *Casta*, race It is especially used by Europeans to denote the different classes into which the Hindus are divided. *Varňa*, colour, and *Játi*, race, are Indian names *Chatúrvarnya*, the country of the four colours, is an ancient distinguishing epithet of India. To the present day, caste is regarded by other nations of the earth as the characteristic feature of the Hindus. In the earlier ages of society the system prevailed extensively throughout the world; but in course of time it was abandoned in all countries except India and Ceylon.

Among no other nation was it ever observed with such strictness or enforced by such severe penalties as among the Hindus. From birth to the funeral pile, it directs every movement. The Hindu, by day and night, at home or abroad, in waking, sleeping, eating, drinking, in all the customs of the society in which he moves and in the events determining his entire life, is always under its pervading and overmastering influence.*

Mr. Wilkins, in his *Modern Hinduism*, makes the following quotation from Dr. Wilson :—

"To give some idea of the minute regulations of this system of caste, and how its laws are framed to regulate the life of its slaves, it may be mentioned that it has for infancy, pupilage, and manhood its ordained methods of sucking, sipping, drinking, and eating, of washing, anointing, of clothing and ornamenting the body; of sitting, rising, reclining; of moving, visiting, travelling, of speaking, reading, listening and reciting; and of meditating, singing, working and fighting. It has its laws for social and religious rites, privileges and occupations; for education, duty, religious service; for errors, sins, transgressions; for intercommunion, avoidance and excommunication; for defilement and purification; for fines and other punishments It unfolds the ways of committing what it calls sins, accumulating sin, and putting away sin, of acquiring, dispensing and losing merit. It treats of inheritance, conveyance, possession, dispossession of property, and of bargains, gains, loss, and ruin. It deals with death, burial and burning, and with commemoration, assistance and injury after death It interferes, in short, with all the relations and events of life, and with what precedes and follows, or what is supposed to precede and follow life. It reigns supreme in

* Sherring's *Hindu Tribes and Castes*.

the innumerable classes and divisions of the Hindus, whether they originate in family descent, in religious opinions, in civil or sacred occupations, or in local residence; and it professes to regulate all their interests, affairs and relationships. Caste is the guiding principle of each of the classes and divisions of the Hindus viewed in their distinct and associated capacity." pp. 125; 6

"That the thoughtful and educated of men of India," says Mr Sherring, "should patiently endure its tyranny—a tyranny the most relentless, and at the same time the most senile and unreasonable ever exercised by the human mind in its greatest corruption—is a phenomenon unparalleled in the history of our race." Even the lowest and most degraded of the people, who are spurned from the temples, are some of them as great sticklers for caste as the highest.

Among the Hindu population in Ceylon, caste is much the same as in India. In a modified form it exists, more or less, among the Sinhalese. Most of the Sinhalese have a very mongrel religion. Demon worship was at first the only superstition, and it still exerts the strongest hold upon them. Buddhism was afterwards introduced; but, though condemned by it, demon worship retained its power. The worship of the Hindu gods and the caste system were introduced from India. The Sinhalese mingle the three. Some of them seek to add a little from Christianity. Only a comparatively small number are sufficiently enlightened to adhere to one religion.

Hindu Caste Peculiar.—It is often alleged that caste distinctions are similar to the civil and social distinctions of European and other nations; but there is an essential difference. Recently it was thus explained by Mr. G. N. Chandavarkar, the Bombay delegate to England :—

"I have heard the question asked by the apologists of caste—'Does not caste exist in England too? Will a lord, generally speaking, not think it degrading to marry a farmer's daughter?' I reply that caste in the form and under the circumstance in which it exists in India does not exist anywhere else. An English lord may, generally speaking, think it degrading to marry a farmer's daughter, but a farmer in England can hope to be a lord himself. What Cardinal Newman says of Christians is true of the English: 'They never pronounce of any one, now external to them, that he will not some day be among them.' In India, on the other hand, a Brahman is a Brahman and a Sudra is a Sudra; the latter can never hope to rise to the level of the former. There is consequently not that bond of 'good fellowship' between the two, and caste has encouraged in India the growth of the principle of what Cardinal Newman calls 'repulsion between man and man.'"

Indian caste is derived from *birth* alone. It cannot be transferred from one class to another; it cannot be gained as a reward for the highest merit or bestowed as an honorary title by the most powerful monarch.* As well might an ass be changed into a horse. The Queen of England can raise any of her subjects to the peerage, but she cannot alter the caste of a Hindu. The highest nobleman in England may enter the cottage of the humblest person in England, and sit with him at table; not so in India.

At the same time, it must be allowed that in England there is far too much pride of rank and wealth. Mr. Justice Talfourd, in some of his last words, lamented "that separation between class and class which is the great curse of British society, and for which we are all, more or less, in our respective spheres, in some degree responsible."

Investigation of Caste.—In former times it was considered sufficient to follow the custom. This led to a stationary condition of society. The present is an age of inquiry. The question regarding every institution is, not whether it is *old*, but whether it is *good?*

Most Indians have very erroneous ideas of the "ancients." They look upon those who lived thousands of years ago as very old and very wise; while the present generation are compared to children. The very contrary is the case. *We are the ancients.* The world is now older by thousands of years; those who lived long ago are like the children. We ought also to be the wiser.

It is granted that institutions and customs, especially those of long standing, should not be condemned or changed without careful consideration and sufficient reasons. The object of the present Paper is to seek to lead Hindus to make this inquiry. When books were comparatively few, existing only in manuscript or shrouded in Sanskrit, any examination of the question was very difficult. Now the principal works bearing on the subject have been printed, and several of them translated into English. Any intelligent person having access to them is able to form his own opinion.

An all-devouring credulity is an attribute of the uneducated Hindu or even one of the Pundit class. The greatest self-contradictions, the wildest tales, do not awaken his common sense. The following remarks are intended only for men trained to weigh evidence and to reason logically. As a rule, authorities are quoted, and, where practicable, the opinions of eminent scholars are given on each point.

---

* The Brahmans have devised a way for the Maharaja of Travancore. He is made a twice-born by passing through a golden cow or lotus. The cow is of the same weight as himself, and is afterwards cut into pieces and distributed among the Brahmans. Probably the same plan would be efficacious in other cases, if people were willing to bear the expense. The Maharaja afterwards cannot eat with the members of his own family, but he is admitted to the high privilege of seeing the Brahmans enjoying their meals, and of eating in their presence.

HINDU ACCOUNTS OF THE ORIGIN OF THE CASTES.

The common belief among the Hindus is that the Brahmans proceeded from the mouth of Brahma, the Kshatriyas from his arms; the Vaishyas from his thighs, and the Sudras from his feet.

Dr. John Muir, a distinguished Sanskrit scholar, devoted great attention to an examination of the Hindu books with regard to the origin of caste. The results are contained in a volume of 532 octavo pages.* Numerous extracts are given in the original Sanskrit, with English translations, of passages bearing on the subject. Only a very few of the principal can be quoted; but the general conclusions at which Dr. Muir arrived will be given.

The learned Dr Wilson of Bombay published a work on Caste in two volumes. Mr. Sherring, of Benares, gave, in three quarto volumes, detailed accounts of the Indian castes The Census Reports also contain more or less information on the subject.

Rig-Veda—The oldest known passage which makes mention of the fourfold origin of the Hindu race is the 90th hymn of the 10th Book, called Purusha Sukta, or the hymn to Purusha.

"1. Purusha has a thousand heads, a thousand eyes, a thousand feet. 6. When the gods performed a sacrifice with Purusha as the oblation, the spring was its butter, the summer its fuel, and the autumn its offering. 7. This victim, Purusha, born in the beginning, they immolated on the sacrificial grass, with him the gods, the Sadhyas, and the rishis sacrificed. 11. When (the gods) divided Purusha, into how many parts did they cut him up? What was his mouth? What arms (had he)? What (two objects) are said (to have been) his thighs and feet? 12. The Brahman was his mouth; the Rajanya was made his arms; the being (called) the Vaisya, he was his thighs; the Sudra sprang from his feet. 13 The moon sprang from his soul, the sun from his eye, Indra and Agni from his mouth, and Vayu from his breath. From his navel arose the air, from his head the sky, from his feet the earth, from his ear the (four) quarters; in this manner (the gods) formed the worlds."

Oriental scholars are agreed that the Vedic hymns were composed at dates widely apart from each other. The general opinion is that the Purusha Sukta is one of the latest, belonging to the Brahmana period.

Satapatha Brahmana—Works of this class, though later, are considered of equal authority with the Vedas. The Satapatha Brahmana gives the following account of the origin of the castes:—

"(Uttering) 'bhuh,' Prajapati generated this earth, (uttering) 'bhuvah,' he generated the air, and (uttering) 'svah,' he generated the sky. Saying 'bhuh,' Prajapati generated the Brahman; (saying) 'bhuvah' he generated the Kshattra; (and saying) 'svah,' he generated the Vis." II. 1, 4.

---

* *Original Sanskrit Texts*, Volume I Mythical and Legendary Accounts of the Origin of Caste, with an Enquiry into its Existence in the Vedic Age Trubner.

Taittiriya Brahmana.—This treatise gives another account:—

"This entire (universe) has been created by Brahma. Men say that the Vaisya class was produced from the Rig Veda. They say that the Yajur Veda is the womb from which the Kshattriya was born. The Sama Veda is the source from which the Brahmans sprang." III, 12, 9

The same Brahmana states elsewhere.—

"The Brahman caste is sprung from the gods, the sudra from the Asuras." I 2, 6, 7.

Manu.—After describing how Brahma, the parent of all worlds, was born in a golden egg, he says:

"31 That the world might be peopled, he caused the Brahman, the Kshatriya, the Vaisya and the Sudra to issue from his mouth, his arms, his thighs, and his feet." Book I.

In the next verse Manu gives a different account.—

"32 Having divided his own body into two, he became a male by half, by half a female: on her that Lord begat Viraj."

"33. But O best of twice-born men! know that I am he, the creator of all this world, whom that male Viraj, having practised austerity, spontaneously produced." Book I

Mahabharata.—In this voluminous work different accounts of the origin of caste may be expected. In the Santi-parva, Bhrigu makes the following statement:—

"There is no difference of castes this world, having been at first created by Brahma entirely Brahmanic, became (afterwards) separated into castes in consequence of works. Those twice-born men who were fond of sensual pleasure, fiery, irascible, prone to violence, who had forsaken their duty and were red-limbed, fell into the condition of Kshatriyas. Those twice-born who derived their livelihood from kine, who were yellow, who subsisted by agriculture and who neglected to practise their duties, entered into the state of Vaisyas. Those twice-born who were addicted to mischief and falsehood, who were covetous, who lived by all kinds of work, who were black and had fallen from purity, sank into the condition of Sudras. Being separated from each other by these works, the Brahmans became divided into different castes."

In the same Santi-parva the creation of the four castes is ascribed to Krishna

"Then, again, the great Krishna created a hundred Brahmans, the most excellent, from his mouth, a hundred Kshatriyas from his arms, a hundred Vaisyas from his thighs, and a hundred Sudras from his feet."

Bhagavad Gita.—Chapter IV. contains the following:—

"The Deity said, 'The fourfold division of castes was created by me according to the apportionment of qualities and duties.'"

These duties are described in Chapter XVIII.

Vishnu Purana—In the 6th Section of Book I, Parasara professes to tell how Brahma formed the human race.—

"3. When true to his design, Brahma became desirous to create the world, creatures in whom goodness (*sattva*) prevailed sprang from his mouth; (4) others in whom passion (*rajas*) predominated came from his breast, others in whom both passion and darkness (*tamas*) were strong, proceeded from his thighs, (5) others he created from his feet, whose chief characteristic was darkness Of these was composed the system of four castes, Brahmans, Kshatriyas, Vaisyas, and Sudras, who had respectively issued from his mouth, breast, thighs, and feet"

Vayu Purana.—The 8th Chapter states that in the Krita Age there was only one caste:—

"62 There were then no distinctions of castes or orders and no mixture of castes. Men acted towards each other without any feeling of love or hatred. 63. In the Krita age they were born alike in form and duration of life, without any distinction of lower and higher"

Bhagavata Purana—The Second Book accepts the usual account of the origin of the castes. The Ninth Book declares that in the Krita Age there was only one caste:—

"There was formerly only one Veda, only one god, Narayana, one Agni and one Caste. From Pururavas came the triple Veda in the beginning of the Treta."

Dr. Muir's Conclusions—After examining many other passages, the results arrived at are briefly the following:—

It is abundantly evident that the sacred books of the Hindus contain no uniform or consistent account of the origin of castes; but, on the contrary, present the greatest varieties of speculation on this subject Explanations mystical, mythical, and rationalistic, are all offered in turn; and the freest scope is given by the individual writers to fanciful and arbitrary conjecture

The most common story is that the castes issued from the mouth, arms, thighs and feet of Purusha, or Brahma. The oldest extant passage in which this idea occurs is found in the Purusha Sukta; but it is doubtful whether, in the form in which it is there presented, this representation is anything more than an allegory. In Manu and the Puranas, the mystical import of the Vedic text disappears, and the figurative narration is hardened into a literal statement of fact.

In other passages when a separate origin is assigned to the castes, they are variously said to have sprung from the words bhuh, bhuvah, svah, from different Vedas; from different sets of prayers, from the gods and the Asuras; from nonentity, from the imperishable, the perishable, and other principles

In the Vishnu, Vayu and Markandeya Puranas, where castes are described as coeval with the creation, we are allowed to infer that during the Krita age the condition of the whole race was one of uniform happiness; while the actual separation into castes did not take place, according to the Vayu Purana, until men had become deteriorated in the Treta age.

In one passage men are said to be the offspring of Vivasvat, in another his son Manu is said to be their progenitor, whilst in a third they are said to be descended from a female of the same name. The passage which declares Manu to have been father of the human race, explicitly affirms that men of all the four castes were descended from him. In another remarkable text the Mahabharata asserts that originally there was no distinction of classes, the existing distribution having arisen out of difference of character and occupation. Similarly, the Bhagavata Purana in one place informs us that in the Krita age there was but one caste.

The very different opinions with regard to the origin of caste are an illustration of the remark in the Mahabharata:

"Contradictory are the Vedas; contradictory are the Shastras; contradictory all the doctrines of the holy sages"

When witnesses in a court of justice give conflicting evidence, discredit is thrown upon all their testimony. Writings cannot be infallible which involve self-contradictions. One would think that no man in his senses would accept the account of creation in the Purusha Sukta as literally true. The old Hindu writers framed their geography and astronomy out of their own heads, and it was much the same with their accounts of the origin of caste. Each one followed his own fancy. However monstrous the fiction, it did not matter. There is a nursery rhyme in England about the cow jumping over the moon. Very young children accept this as true, and most Hindus are just as credulous.

TRUE ORIGIN OF CASTE

The second volume of Dr. Muir's *Original Sanskrit Texts* shows, by numerous quotations, that the Aryan Hindus are of "Trans-Himalayan Origin and akin to the Western Branches of the Indo-European Race" This is fully admitted by Indian scholars. Professor Bhandarkar said at Bombay:

"Europeans have successfully traced the affinity of the Sanskrit with the ancient languages of Europe, and shown that the Aryans of India, composed of the three castes, Brahman, Kshatriya and Vais'ya, belong to the same race as the ancient Greeks and Romans and the nations of modern Europe except the Turks, the Hungarians and the Fins"

Professor Max Müller, in his *Chips from a German Workshop*, has an admirable review of Dr. Muir's work. The following remarks are chiefly abridged from these two writers.

Caste arose from two chief causes: 1. Difference of Race. 2. Difference of employment. Locality is a third element of minor importance, which will be noticed under the second head.

1. Difference of Race.

The ordinary names for caste prove this. *Játi* means race, *varna*, colour, arising from difference of race.

In the Vedas there are only two castes,—the *Aryas* and the *Dasyus*. A short account will be given of each.

Aryas.—This word, meaning noble, probably comes from *ar*, to plough,—the nations following agriculture being more civilised than the wandering races.

At very early period a tribe speaking a language not yet Sanskrit or Greek, or German, settled in the highlands of Central Asia. As they multiplied, more land was needed for cultivation, fresh pastures for their cattle. In search of these, bands went off at different times. The main stream flowed towards the north-west. The earliest to migrate were the ancestors of the Celts, who probably found Europe a jungle, traversed by wandering tribes. They were followed by the ancestors of the Italians, Greeks, Germans, and Slavonians.

"The Hindu," says Max Muller, "though perhaps the eldest, was the last to leave the central home of the Aryan family. He saw his brothers all depart towards the setting sun, and then turning towards the south and east, he started alone in search of a new world."

Language proves that, without doubt, the ancestors of the principal nations of Europe and the Hindus once dwelt together.

"The terms for God, for house, for father, mother, son and daughter, for dog and cow, for heart and tears, for axe and tree, identical in all the Indo-European idioms, are like the watchwords of soldiers. We challenge the seeming stranger; and whether he answer with the lips of a Greek, a German, or an Indian, we recognise him as one of ourselves. There *was* a time when the ancestors of the Celts, the Germans, the Slavonians, the Greeks and Italians, the Persians and Hindus, were living together within the same fences, separate from the ancestors of the Semitic and Turanian races."*

The Aryans were then no longer dwellers in tents, but builders of permanent houses. As the name for king is the same in Sanskrit, Latin, Teutonic, and Celtic, we know that kingly government was established and recognised by the Aryans at the prehistoric period.

* Max Muller.

They also worshipped an unseen Being, under the self-same name. We have in the Veda the invocation *Dyaus pitar*, the Greek *Zeu páter*, the Latin *Jupiter*, and that means in all the three languages what it meant before these three languages were torn asunder—it means Heaven-Father!

Hence the European, whom the Hindu regards as an unclean Mlechcha, is a long separated brother, who once dwelt with him in the same mountain home, speaking the same language, and worshipping the same God.

The Aryas, descending the passes of the Hindu Kush, slowly migrated towards India by Kabul Like many succeeding invaders, they probably crossed the Indus at Attock. The tribes which they found occupying the country will next be described.

Dasyus—This name was applied by the Aryas to the aborigines of India whom they sought to dispossess of their lands. The word is supposed to mean *enemies*. So many of them were enslaved that the word *dasa* was applied to a servant. They also so frequently plundered their conquerors, that long afterwards their name was employed as the common term to describe a prowling robber.

The Dasyus were non-Aryan tribes. Remains of them are still found all over India. The main body was driven to the south, and to the present day all the languages spoken there, Tamil, Telugu, Canarese, &c., are distinct from the Sanskrit.

The Aryas, coming from a cool climate, were fairer in complexion than the Dasyus. The Aryas prided themselves on their colour, and called the Dasyus "the black skin," just as some ignorant, vulgar Europeans of the present day call Hindus "niggers" The noses of the Dasyus were not so prominent as those of the Aryas. Hence the Dasyus were described as "goat-nosed" and "noseless," whereas the Aryan gods are frequently praised for their beautiful noses.

In other passages of the Vedas, the Dasyus are represented as keeping no sacred fires, and as worshipping mad gods. Nay, they are even taunted with eating raw flesh, and with feeding on human flesh. The following are Vedic invocations with regard to the Dasyus.—

"Indra and Soma, burn the devils, destroy them, throw them down, ye two Bulls, the people that grow in darkness! Hew down the madmen, suffocate them, kill them; hurl them away, and slay the voracious.

"Indra and Soma, up together against the cursing demon! May he burn and hiss like an oblation in the fire! Put your everlasting hatred upon the villain who hates the Brahman, who eats flesh, and whose look is abominable."

Some, at least, of the Dasyus, were not so barbarous as they are represented by the Aryas. The wealth of the Dasyus is spoken of in several places; *e.g.* "Subdue the might of the Dasa; may we through Indra divide his collected wealth." They had forts and cities. "Indra and Agni, by one effort together ye have shattered 90 forts belonging to the Dasyus." "O Indra, impetuous, thou didst shatter by thy bolt 99 cities for Puru."

The following is abridged from Dr. Muir:—

We may conceive the Aryas proceeding from the Indus in a south-easterly direction into a country probably covered with forest, and occupied by tribes of a dark complexion, speaking a strange language. The Aryas, meanwhile, as they advanced, and gradually established themselves in the forests, fields and villages of the aborigines, would not be able at once to secure their position, but would be exposed to constant reprisals on the part of their enemies, who would avail themselves of every opportunity to assail them, to carry off their cattle, disturb their rites, and impede their progress The black complexion, barbarous habits, rude speech, and savage yells of the Dasyus, and the sudden attacks under cover of the unpenetrable forests and the darkness of night, they would make on the encampments of the Aryas, might naturally lead the latter to speak of them as demons.

The Aryas, after advancing some way, would halt to occupy, to clear and cultivate the territory they had acquired; and the aborigines would continue in possession of the adjacent tracts, sometimes at peace, and sometimes at war with their invaders At length the further advance of the Aryas would either drive the Dasyus into the remotest corners of the country or would lead to their partial incorporation with the conquerors as the lowest grade in their community.

The first great distinction was between the white and dark races, the conquerors and the conquered, the freeman and the slave. The Sudras undoubtedly were the aboriginal races of India subdued by the Aryan invaders. One of the earliest tribes brought under subjection was called *Sudras*, and this name was extended to the whole race.

"This ancient division between Aryan and non-Aryan races, based on an original difference of blood, was preserved in later times as the primary distinction between the three twice-born castes and the Sudras. The word ârya (noble) is derived from ărya, which means householder, and was originally used as the name of the third caste, or the Vaisyas. These Aryas, or Vaisyas, formed the great bulk of the Brahmanic society, and it is but natural that their name, in a derivative form, should have been used as a common name of the three classes into which these Aryans became afterwards divided"*

* *Chips from a German Workshop*, Vol. II. The other quotations are from the same work

II. DIFFERENCE OF EMPLOYMENT AND LOCALITY.

"The three occupations of the Aryans in India were fighting, cultivating the soil, and worshipping the gods. Those who fought the battles of the people would naturally acquire influence and rank, and their leaders appear in the Veda as Rajas or kings. Those who did not share in the fighting would occupy a more humble position; they were called Vis, Vaisyas, or householders, and would no doubt have to contribute towards the maintenance of the armies. But a third occupation, that of worshipping the gods, was evidently considered by the whole nation to be as important and as truly essential to the well-being of the country, as fighting against enemies or cultivating the soil."

"No nation was ever so anxious to perform the service of their gods as the early Hindus. It is the gods who conquer the enemy, it is the gods who vouchsafe a rich harvest Health and wealth, children, friends, flocks and gold are all the gifts of the gods. Among a nation of this peculiar stamp the priests were certain to acquire great influence at a very early period, and like most priests, they were as certain to use it for their own advantage."

At first any one might preside at a sacrifice. Great importance was attached to the hymns which were sung. "A hymn by which the gods had been invoked at the beginning of a battle, and which had secured to the king a victory over his enemies, was considered an unfailing spell, and it became the sacred war-song of a whole tribe." These hymns were handed down from father to son as the most valuable heir-loom. Writing was then unknown. A knowledge of the hymns was confined to a certain class who "impressed the people with the belief that the slightest mistake in the words or in the pronunciation of the words,* would rouse the anger of the gods. Thus they became masters of all religious ceremonies, the teachers of the people, the ministers of kings. Their favour was courted, their anger dreaded, by a pious but credulous race"

The Brahman was at first simply an assistant at sacrifices, by whom or for whom conducted. Afterwards he became a *purohita* (one set in front) or family priest. This office became hereditary, and those who held at courts became the advisers and counsellors of kings. Such a post was peculiarly favourable to the designs of a crafty and ambitious priest, and must have offered him exceptional opportunities for promoting the hierarchical aspirations of his order.

The Aitareya Brahmana says, "Verily the gods do not eat the food offered by the king who is without a purohita; wherefore let the

---

* The priests, among the old Romans, to acquire greater power for themselves, taught the same. Hence a sacrifice had sometimes to be repeated thirty times on account of mistakes made. Even pause in the music at a wrong time, required the whole to be begun afresh

king, who wishes to sacrifice, place a Brahman at the head." VIII. 24, 25.

In the Veda we still find kings composing their own hymns to the gods, royal bards, Rajarishis, who united in their person the powers both of king and priest. The family of Visvamitra has contributed its own collection of hymns to the Rig-Veda; but Visvamitra himself was a Kshatriya. If in later times he is represented as admitted into the Brahmanic family of the Brigus, this is but an excuse invented by the Brahmans, in order to explain what would otherwise have upset their own system. Visvamitra was the author of the Gayatri. Professor Bhattacharjya says, "What more convincing evidence could there be of the exceedingly small importance attached to caste in the Rig-Veda time, than that the holiest text in the whole body of the Veda should have been attributed to a member of the Kshatriya tribe?"*

King Janaka is represented in some of the Brahmanas as more learned than any of the Brahmans at his court. He also asserted his right of performing sacrifices without the intervention of priests. Manu, the most famous legislator, too, was by birth a Kshatriya

As the influence of the Brahmans extended, they became more and more jealous of their privileges, and, while fixing their own claims, they endeavoured at the same time to circumscribe the duties of the warriors and householders. Those of the Aryas who would not submit to the laws of the three estates were treated as outcasts, and they were chiefly known by the name of Vratyas, or tribes. The aboriginal inhabitants, again, who conformed to the Brahmanic law, received certain privileges, and were constituted a fourth caste, under the name of Sudras, whereas all the rest who kept aloof were called Dasyus (Manu x. 45)

This Brahmanic constitution, however, was not settled in a day, and we find everywhere in the hymns, in the Brahmanas, and in the epic poems, the traces of a long-continued warfare between the Aryas and the aboriginal inhabitants, and violent contests between the two highest classes of the Aryans striving for political supremacy. For a long time the three upper classes continued to consider themselves as one race, all claiming the title of Arya, in contradistinction from the fourth caste, or the Sudras.

After long and violent struggles between the Brahmans and the Kshatriyas, the Brahmans carried the day, and, if we may judge from the legends which they themselves have preserved of those struggles, they ended with the total destruction of most of the old Kshatriya families, and the admission of a few of them to the privileges of the first caste. Parusu-rama is the great hero of the Brahmans.

* *Tagore Law Lectures*, p. 110

"He cleared the earth thrice seven times of the Kshatriya caste, and filled with their blood the five large lakes of Samanta, from which he offered libations to the race of Bhrigu. Offering a solemn sacrifice to the king of the gods, Parasu-rama presented the earth to the ministering priests Having given the earth to Kasyapa, the hero of immeasurable prowess, retired to the Mohendra mountain, where he still resides; and in this manner was there enmity between him and the race of the Kshatriyas, and thus was the whole earth conquered by Parasu-rama."*

This account of the struggle is grossly exaggerated, and it is difficult to say how much truth there is in it.

By the time of Manu, however, the Brahmans were high above the Kshatriyas before whom, but a few centuries earlier, they had cringed and fawned.

Manu's explanation of the Mixed Castes—Manu represents the various castes as the result of mixed marriages between the four original castes. According to him, the four primitive castes, by intermarrying in every possible way, gave rise to 16 mixed castes, which by continuing their intermarriages produced the long list of the mixed castes.

If we look more carefully, says Max Muller, we shall find that most of these mixed castes are in reality the professions, trades, and guilds of a half-civilised society. They did not wait for mixed marriages before they came into existence. Professions, trades and handicrafts had grown up without any reference to caste. Some of their names were derived from towns and countries where certain professions were held in particular estimation. Servants who waited on ladies were called Vaidehas, because they came from Videha. In other cases the names of Manu's castes were derived from their occupations The caste of musicians, for instance, were called *Venas* from *vina*, the lyre. Now it was evidently Manu's object to bring these professional corporations in connection with the old system of castes, assigning to each, according to its higher or lower position, a more or less pure descent from the original castes. The Vaidyas, for instance, or the physicians, evidently a respectable corporation, were represented as the offspring of a Brahman father and a Vaisya mother, while the guild of the fishermen, or Nishadas, were put down as the descendants of a Brahman father and a Sudra mother.

Thus a new system of caste came in of a purely professional character, though artificially grafted on the rotten trunk of the ancient castes. This is the system which is still in force in India, and which has exercised its influence on the state of Indian society for good and evil.

Dr. Cornish takes the same view as professor Max Müller, and gives the explanation of Manu's system :—

"No dependence can be placed on Manu's authority for the origin of

* *Chips*, Vol II.

these mixed castes. Such people existed in his time, and their existence had to be accounted for, and it is always an easier thing for a Hindu author to make fanciful assertions than to adhere to the sober domain of fact, and hence probably the wonderful legends of their origin from certain mixtures of castes"

"It is characteristic of the Brahmanical intolerance of the compilers of the code that the origin of the lowest of all (*the Chandála*) should be ascribed to the intercourse of a Sudra man and Brahman woman, while the union of a Brahman male with a Sudra woman is said to have resulted in one of the highest of the mixed classes Indeed it was quite lawful in ancient times for a Brahman to take a succession of wives from the inferior castes

"The object of the regulations regarding admixture of castes seems to have been to visit with the heaviest pains and penalties any irregularities of the *females* of the twice-born castes, and their degradation, and that of their offspring, for unions with inferior or impure castes, and consequently in the origin of mixed castes, Manu assigns to the offspring of the Brahman woman the lowest degradation of all

"Again, the Chunchu or Chentsu, a race of hunters and forest men, are spoken of by Manu as 'sons of Brahmans by women of the Vaideha class,' whereas these identical people exist to this day, as they had existed probably thousands of years before the caste system was known, as an aboriginal people living in forests, subsisting on the products of the chase, and such roots and vegetable substances as require no cultivation. The whole of the chapter relating to mixed castes is so puerile in tone, and shows so much of class hatred and intolerance, it gives such freedom of intercourse to Brahmans without disqualification, and heaps such dreadful penalties on the incontinence of Brahman women, that the object of the compilers is at once apparent. It is plain that the account of the origin of mixed castes is entirely fanciful, and that not the smallest reliance can be placed on the authority.

"The whole caste system, as it has come down to us, bears unmistakeable evidence of Brahmanical origin."*

"Men who have the same interests, the same occupations, the same principles, unite in self-defence, and after acquiring power and influence they not only defend their rights, but claim important privileges. They naturally impose upon their members certain rules which are considered essential to the interest of their caste or company. These rules, sometimes of apparently the most trifling character, are observed by individual members with greater anxiety than even the laws of religion, because an offence against the latter may be pardoned, while a disregard of the former would lead to an instant exclusion or loss of caste. The more lucrative the trade, the more jealously it was guarded, and there was evidently no trade in India so lucrative as that of the priests. The priests were, therefore, the strongest advocates of the system of caste, and

* *Madras Census Report* for 1871, pp 122, 123

after investing it with a sacred character in the eyes of the people, they expanded it into an immense spider's web, which separated class from class, family from family, man from man, and which, while it rendered all united action impossible, enabled the watchful priests to pounce upon all who dread to disturb the threads of their social tissue and to wither them to death."*

Manu's account of the supposed multiplication of castes is just as mythical as that of the supposed origin of the four castes from Brahma. The longer quotation from the Mahabharata gives the true explanation—it arose from difference of employment

When the Brahmans could not extirpate the worship of the aboriginal demons, they adopted them, calling them incarnations of some of their gods. In like manner, they have connected different occupations with their caste system.

Mr. Sherring thus explains how subdivisions of castes may have taken place:

"The caste separated into clans, each of which managed its own affairs, held *panchayets* or councils, and maintained a distinct and independent existence. As these clans were not amenable to one another or to the caste itself considered as a federal whole, gradually they became jealous of each other's rights, and at length, impelled by the national habit of exclusiveness, abandoned one another reciprocally, and assumed to themselves absolutely all the functions and prerogatives of castes."†

The *Amrita Bazar Patrika* attributes many of the subdivisions to jealousy between rival families:

"The principal cause of the multiplication of castes is continual quarrel and misunderstanding among men holding a certain degree of social rank"

To the foregoing, Sir A. C. Lyall would add, as a source of Indian caste, Sectarian differences, "meaning the castes which are produced by difference of religion, by new gods, new rites, new views, and new dogmas."‡

THE LAWS OF CASTE ACCORDING TO MANU.

The *Ordinances of Manu* constitute the highest authority for the laws of Hindu caste. It is not certain when this work was composed. Mr. Siromani says:—

"There is a tradition that Manu has undergone three successive redactions. The introduction to Narada states that the work of Manu origin-

* Nearly the whole of this section, except where otherwise stated, is from professor Max Muller

† *Hindu Tribes and Castes.* Introduction Vol. II. xxii.

‡ *Asiatic Studies*, p 5

ally consisted of 1,000 chapters and 100,000 slokas; Narada abridged it to 12,000 slokas, and Sumati again reduced it to 4,000. The treatise which we possess must be a third abridgment, as it only extends to 2,685."*

Manu's regulations give the ideal of government and justice according to the Brahmans. The work is so extensive that only a few quotations can be made.

Brahmans.

Their Claims.

92. Man is declared purer above the navel; therefore the purest (part) of him is said by the Self-Existent to be his mouth.

93 Since he sprang from the most excellent part, since he was the first-born, and since he holds the Vedas, the Brahman is, by right, the lord of all this creation.

94 Him the Self-Existent, after having performed penance, created in the beginning from his own mouth, for presentation of oblations to the gods and offerings to the manes, (and) for the preservation of all this (world.)

95 What being is there superior to him, by whose mouth the gods eat oblations and the manes offerings?

98. The birth of a Brahman is a perpetual incarnation of *dharma*; for he exists for the sake of *dharma*, and is for the existence of the Vedas.

99. When the Brahman is born, he is born above the world, the chief of all creatures, to guard the treasury of *dharma*.

100. Thus whatever exists in the universe is all the property of the Brahman; for the Brahman is entitled to all by his superiority and eminence of birth.

101 The Brahman eats his own alone, wears his own, and gives away his own; through the benevolence of the Brahman, indeed, the other people enjoy (all they have)." Book I.

Punishment of Brahmans.

379. Shaving the head is ordained as (the equivalent of) capital punishment in the case of a Brahman, but in the case of the other castes capital punishment may be (inflicted).

380. Certainly (the king) should not slay a Brahman even if he be occupied in crime of every sort; but he should put him out of the realm in possession of all his property, and uninjured (in body).

381. No greater wrong is found on earth than killing a Brahman; therefore the king should not even mentally consider his death" Bk VIII.

The atonement for killing a Sudra is the same as for killing the following animals:

132. On killing a cat, an ichneumon, a daw, or a frog, a dog, a lizard, an owl, or a crow, he should practise the observance (ordained for) killing a Sudra. Book XI.

---

* *Commentary on the Hindu Law* p 16

SUDRAS.

Created for Servitude.

91. One duty the Lord assigned to a Sudra—service to those (before mentioned) classes, without grudging. Book I.

413. But a Sudra, whether bought or not bought, (the Brahman) may compel to practise servitude; for that (Sudra) was created by the Self-existent merely for the service of the Brahman.

414. Even if freed by his master, the Sudra is not released from servitude; for this (servitude) is innate in him: who then can take it from him?

410. The king should . . . make the Sudra (act) as the slave of those who are twice-born. Book VIII.

123. Merely to serve the Brahmans is declared (to be) the most excellent occupation of a Sudra; for if he does anything other than this, it profits him nothing.

129. Indeed, an accumulation of wealth should not be made by a Sudra even (if he is) able (to do so), for a Sudra getting possession of wealth merely injures the Brahmans. Book X.

417. A Brahman may take possession of the goods of a Sudra with perfect peace of mind, for, since nothing at all belongs to this (Sudra) as his own, he is one whose property may be taken away by his master." Book VIII.

Reward of Servitude.

125. The leavings of food should be given (him) and the old clothes; so too the blighted part of the grain; so too the old furniture." Book X.

Punishment of Sudras.

270. If a (man) of one birth assault one of the twice-born castes with virulent words, he ought to have his tongue cut out, for he is of the lowest origin.

271. If he make mention in an insulting manner of their name and caste, a red-hot iron rod, ten fingers long, should thrust into his mouth.

272. If this man through insolence gives instruction to the priests in regard to their duty, the king should cause boiling hot oil to be poured into his mouth and ear.

279. If a man of the lowest birth should with any member injure one of the highest station, even that member of this man shall be cut (off): this is an ordinance of Manu.

280. If he lift up his hand or his staff (against him), he ought to have his hand cut off; and if he smites him with his foot in anger, he ought to have his foot cut off.

281. If a low-born man endeavours to sit down by the side of a high-born man, he should be banished after being branded on the hip, or (the king) may cause his backside to be cut off.

282. If through insolence he spit upon him, the king should cause his two lips to be cut off.

283 If he seize him by the locks, let the king without hesitation cause both his hands to be cut off Book VIII.

Treatment of certain Castes.

51 The dwelling of Chandalas and Swapacas (should be) outside the village; they should be deprived of dishes, their property (consists of) dogs and asses

52 Their clothes (should be) the garments of the dead, and their food (should be) in broken dishes, their ornaments (should be) of iron; and they must constantly wander about

53. A man who practises the rule of right should not desire intercourse with these (people); their business transactions must be among each other; their marriages (should be only) with their equals.

54. Their food (for which they are) dependent on others should be given in a broken dish, they should not wander by night among the villages and towns." Book X.

Sudras not to receive Religious Instruction.

80. One may not give advice to a Sudra, nor (give him) the remains (of food) or (of) butter that has been offered. And one may not teach him the law or enjoin upon him (religious) observances.

81. For he who tells him the law and he who enjoins upon him (religious) observances, he indeed, together with that (Sudra), sinks into the darkness of the hell called Asamvrtta (unbounded) Book IV

The 2,685 verses in Manu's Ordinances contain some rules which are good, many frivolous, and others bad. The foregoing extracts give the spirit of the laws regulating caste.

BUDDHIST OPPOSITION TO CASTE.

Gautama, the founder of Buddhism, is supposed to have lived about the sixth century B. C He was a Kshatriya and freely admitted all castes into his priesthood In the Dhamma Pada, "Footsteps of Religion," he thus describes the true Brahman.—

"391. Him I call indeed a Brahmana who does not offend by body, word, or thought, and is controlled on these three points.

"393. A man does not become a Brahman by his platted hair, by his family, or by birth · in whom there is truth and righteousness he is blessed, he is a Brahmana.

"407. Him I call indeed a Brahman from whom anger and hatred, pride and envy have dropt like mustard seed from the point of a needle."

Pandit Ashwaghosha, a learned Buddhist of Nepal, wrote a Sanskrit treatise, called *Vajra Suchi,* the Needle of Adamant, exposing caste. Some of his arguments will be noticed hereafter.

"Throughout the whole of the Buddhist period in India," says Sherring, "of a thousand years and upwards, strong opposition was cherished, by the Buddhists against caste. During the dominancy of their religion, which lasted perhaps six or seven hundred years, caste was necessarily in a very depressed state; and people generally enjoyed a condition of social freedom which they had not enjoyed, since the earliest ages of Hinduism."

CASTE REVIVAL.

Jainism is closely allied to Buddhism, and the two prevailed extensively throughout India for several centuries. The revival of Hinduism was largely owing to Sankara Acharya, who is supposed to have lived about the ninth century of the Christian era. He was a native of Malabar on the West Coast, of the tribe of Namburi Brahmans. He travelled all over India, engaging in successful controversy with Buddhists and Jains or with Hindu sects. In Malabar he is said to have divided the four original tribes into 72, or 18 subdivisions of each, and to have assigned to them their respective rites and duties.

It is generally supposed that Buddhism and Jainism were extirpated by severe persecution. Madhava Acharya relates how his royal follower Sudhawan, a prince in Southern India, "commanded his servants to put to death the old men and children of the Buddhists from the bridge of Rama to the Snowy Mountains; let him who slays not be slain." In Hindu temples in South India may be seen representations of Buddhists and Jains impaled, with dogs licking the blood which trickles down. The Hindu account is that they seated themselves on the stakes rather than renounce their faith.

There were certainly local struggles; but whether there was any general persecution may be doubted.

The Brahmans, on regaining their supremacy, made the caste rules more stringent than ever. Marriages which were freely permitted by Manu were forbidden. The facility for intermarriage has given place to rigid exclusiveness, so that it is now absolutely impossible for the pure castes to intermarry with the mixed, or for the mixed to intermarry with one another.

Not only is intermarriage between different castes forbidden, but the same castes are split up into numerous subdivisions, which keep nearly as much aloof from one another as if they were distinct castes. Mr. Sherring, in his work on *Hindu tribes and Castes,* enumerates nearly 2,000 subdivisions of Brahmans. Sir W. W. Hunter says, "They follow every employment from the calm *pandits* of Behár in their stainless white robes or the haughty priests of Benares, to the potato-growing Brahmans of Orissa, 'half-naked peasants struggling along under their baskets of yams, with a filthy little Brahmanical thread over their shoulder "*

Mr. Sherring thus describes the divisions among the Brahmans :—

"Hundreds of these tribes, if not at enmity with one another, cherish mutual distrust and antipathy to such a degree that they are socially separated from one another as far as it is possible for them to be,—neither eating nor drinking together, nor intermarrying, and only agreed in matters of religion and in the determination to maintain the pride and secular dominancy of their order. The Brahmans display all the vices of a family divided against itself with more than ordinary intensity, for each one presumes on his purity of caste and birth, and affects the airs and ostentation of an eldest son and heir."

The five tribes of Brahmans in the north, known as Gour, would be excommunicated if they partook of a meal sitting together on the same carpet.

Sir W. W. Hunter says · "In 1864, I saw a Brahman felon try to starve himself to death, and submit to a flogging rather than eat his food on account of scruples as to whether the birthplace of North-Western Brahman, who had cooked it, was equal in sanctity to his own native district."

The Kshatriyas reckon 590 separate tribes. Even the very lowest castes have their subdivisions. Mr. Sherring says .—

"The curse of Brahmanism has fallen on all native society and blighted it. Each caste, down to the lowest, is eaten up with self-satisfaction and self-admiration Indeed, it is a notorious fact that the most debased castes yield to none in the punctilious strictness with which they observe caste prejudices and carry out caste regulations."

In some respects, however, caste has been relaxed under British rule and Western civilization. It is elastic, and adapts itself to the inevitable

---

EFFECTS OF CASTE.

Division of labour exists in all civilised countries. Priests, soldiers, merchants, farmers, mechanics, and servants, are found in every one of them. It is *Hindu Caste*, a peculiar system, which has now to be considered. Its good and bad features, real or supposed, will be noticed in turn

---

* Hunter's *Gazetteer of India.*

ADVANTAGES OF CASTE.

The following seem to be the principal .—

1. **Division of labour secures a certain degree of Excellence.**—A savage who does everything for himself can never rise in civilization. It marks a distinct advance when there are separate professions. The knowledge and skill acquired by the father descend to the son.

2 **Some measure of Protection**—Caste, as it were, makes a man a member of a larger family, having the same interests, and bound to help one another.

3. **Cleanliness**—This is undoubtedly promoted to some extent, by the care about utensils, bathing, &c. Some Indian houses are beautifully clean.

4. **Respect for Authority.**—This was one characteristic of the Hindus in former times. At present, not unfrequently, *insolence* is mistaken for *independence*.

5. **Moral Restraint**—The moral code of Hindu caste greatly differs from modern ideas, as will afterwards be mentioned; but it acts as a check in certain directions and upon certain classes

To the above, Sir Lepel Griffin would add its value in a political point of view to the British Government:

"If England continue to rule with justice, moderation, and impartiality, with clean hands and an honest and eager desire to work for the good of the people, there is no fear that the Hindus will ever turn against her And the explanation of this security is chiefly to be found in caste, which, by depriving the people of ambition, has left each man content with his position in life. Last year, Mr. Lowell, the late American Minister, told us that one of the advantages of democracy was that it enabled a man to 'climb from a coal-pit to the highest position for which he was fitted' But in India, fortunately for society and the government, the collier would have no inclination to climb at all. Every occupation, even thieving, is hereditary; and the rules of caste ordinarily compel a man to follow the occupation of his forefather, except where English influence and education have displaced the conservative tradition in a favor of a more democratic view of the rights of humanity. But the English embroidery is only upon the hem of the mysterious garment of Indian life, and the great mass of the people are unaffected by the struggles of the young men of our schools and colleges to obtain a share in the offices at the disposal of Government Even with these, the spirit of caste is still strong, and a wise policy would encourage and not stifle it"*

There is, however, another side of the picture which will now be given.

---

* *Asiatic Quarterly Review*, Vol. I p 467

Disadvantages of Caste.

The following may be mentioned :—

1. **Physical Degeneracy.**—West, an English physician, author of one of the best treatises on the "Diseases of Children," says, "*First* among the causes of sickly infancy and premature death may be mentioned the intermarriage of near relatives." The Hindus have been split up into probably about a lakh of subdivisions, each holding itself aloof from all others. Professor Ranganatha Mudaliyar gives the following illustration.—

"I am sure I am not guilty of exaggeration when I say that the Mudaliars residing in Madras are divided into as many as fifty sections, no one of which can intermarry with any other The same difficulty of intermarriage exists among Nayudus, and Pillais, and Reddis. It is needless to expatiate on the evil, in a physiological and social point of view, of marriages being contracted between parties so closely related, and of the choice of a husband or wife being confined within such narrow limits"

Caste is also mainly responsible for another cause of physical degeneracy—early marriages. A Bengali defender of caste in the *Calcutta Review* says, "One thing is quite clear, if girls be not married early enough, there can be no certainty that they won't marry outside the caste community."

2. **National Poverty.**—Three causes of this may be mentioned.

1. *Restriction on foreign commerce by forbidding to leave India* — One of the wealthiest cities in ancient time was Tyre, on the eastern coast of the Mediterranean It was built on a small island, connected with the mainland, and had only a few miles of territory. The prophet Ezekiel says of it, "When thy wares went forth out of the seas, thou filledst many people; thou didst enrich the kings of the earth with the multitude of thy riches and of thy merchandise." Isaiah characterises it as, "The crowning city, whose merchants are princes, whose traffickers are the honourable of the earth."

In modern times, England is, perhaps, the richest country in the world One great cause of this is her commerce. Every sea is traversed by her ships; her merchants are to be found in every land where wealth can be gained.

The great Creator intended that there should be free intercourse between the different nations of the earth. Nearly every country is noted for some article of produce. By interchange each is benefited.

Caste teaches the people of India to regard all beyond their own country as impure Mlechchas, and threatens with expulsion any who dare cross "the black water." As far as it has power, caste seeks to prevent the people from gaining the wealth which results from foreign commerce. The Parsis are wiser. Parsi merchants are to be found in London and China, thus largely increasing their business and their profits.

2. *Caste tends to make professions hereditary.*—The late Dr. Krishna Mohan Banerjea says, "The Hindus improved their arts, sciences, and social institutions up to a certain point; they left some of their neighbours behind them in the scale of civilization, —and there they stopped. Their caste prevented the full development of their faculties." Professor Bhandarkar said in Bombay, "Indian implements and arts are now in that condition in which they were in the time of Manu." For three thousand years the Indian plough has been little better than a crooked stick. Caste leads to a stationary civilization. In England some of the greatest improvements in the arts have been made by men who did not belong to the trade, as cotton-spinning and the steam-engine.

3. *Caste makes labour degrading.*—England owes her wealth perhaps even more to her manufactures than her commerce, though they are mutually helpful. The Rev Dr. K. M. Banerjea may again be quoted: "In civilized countries, every encouragement is held out to the cultivators of the arts, especially the fine arts. Their professions are esteemed honourable—their labours are amply rewarded by men of taste and refinement ...The pernicious system of caste taught a different lesson to the Hindus. The civil architect is branded as a bastard The carpenter and the goldsmith are accursed, because the Brahmans chose to take umbrage at them. How could the arts flourish in such a society? How could a person of sensibility aspire to distinction in the cultivation of arts which are considered so low?"

Dr. Banerjea quotes from the Brahma Vaibartha Purana the reasons why certain castes were degraded.

Carpenter.—Born from Vishvakarma and a Sudra mother. Degraded by the curse of the Brahmans, whom he did not readily supply with wood necessary for a burnt offering.

Painter.—Vishvakarma and Sudra mother. Degraded by the curse of the Brahmans for his faults in painting.

Goldsmith.—Degraded by the curse of the Brahman for stealing gold belonging to Brahmans.

Civil Architect.—Born of a painter and Sudra harlot. Degraded because base-born.

Mlechcha—Born of a Khastriya father and Sudra mother. Begotten on a forbidden day. Mlechchas are further described as "People born without the precincts of the 'excellent land of India,' whose ears are not bored, who are cruel, daring, invincible in battle, impure in practice, violent and without religion."* "In their country the regenerate must not even temporarily dwell."

There is an Indian proverb to the effect, that by two things you can distinguish a bullock from a ploughman,—by its horns and its tail. The country is being flooded with candidates for Govenment office, who are mere *consumers*—not *producers*. Improved agriculture, developed manufactures, and foreign commerce, are the real ways by which India may be enriched, but caste discourages or forbids them all.

3. **Intellectual Progress hindered.**—A Bengali writer on caste thus shows how this result was produced:—

"None but a Brahman, declared the Shastras, should read the Veds, or impart religious instruction, and as the Veds and their Angas included all the literature and sciences of the country—grammar, versification, arithmetic, and mathematics—the law thus effectually enjoined ignorance to the rest of mankind. The consequence has been a total prostration of intellect and of mental energy, not only in the general mass of the community, but even among that favoured class itself. Learning has dwindled down to childish frivolity, and religion to ceremonial purity. Our Pandits of the present day are a set of lazy, superstitious weak-minded men, living mostly on the community, without contributing at all to its welfare; having, some of them a little dexterity in threading the dreams of metaphysics, and the unenviable ability of framing specious arguments for perplexing the plainest truths. The cause of so much deterioration is easily explained. When literature and the sciences were ensured in perpetuity to the Brahmans, it became no longer their interest to acquire real knowledge, and the means of making themselves and their brethren wiser and happier. The arts of imposition held out to them more lucrative employment. To cheat and delude the mass, whom the laws had consigned to ignorance and misery, promised them palpable advantages; and they possessed by birthright the means of deceiving with impunity. The temptation was too great for human nature to resist, and it was not resisted."

Brahmans who have not had the advantage of English education are, as a rule, the foes of social progress. They are utterly narrow-minded. They believe that the whole circle of human knowledge is contained in Sanskrit writings, and the most bigoted of them are fully persuaded that to learn anything beyond the Sastras is quite useless.†

For every Brahman in India there are at least twenty members of other castes. All these, according to caste, are doomed, more or less, to ignorance. God has not limited intellectual gifts to one small section of the community. Bunyan, author of the *Pilgrim's Progress*, was a tinker; Burns, the Scottish poet, was a ploughman, Jeremy Taylor, one of the greatest English divines, was the son

* Hindu Caste, pp 25, 26 † Sir Monier Williams, *Modern India*, p. 287.

of a barber, as was Lord Tenterden, a distinguished English lawyer; Shakespeare was the son of a butcher; the author of the Tamil *Kurral*, probably the best ethical poem ever written in India, was a Pariah. If learning is confined to the few, the rich talents which may exist in the many are undeveloped.

4. **Hostility to Social Reform.**—What are the leading social evils under which India is suffering? The neglect of female education, early marriages, the treatment of widows, and the enormous expenses of caste feasts. Caste lies at the root of all, and is the great obstacle to reform. The following extract is from the *Indu Prakash*:—

"Does a Brahman wish to marry his daughter at a mature and marriageable age? There comes the tyrant caste and says, 'You shall not keep your daughter unmarried beyond the age of 8 or 10, unless you choose to incur the penalty of excommunication.' Does a man wish to countenance either by deed or word the marriage of little girls plunged into life-long misery and degrading widowhood? Caste says, 'No, you will be excommunicated.' Does a man wish to dispense with any of the unmeaning and idolatrous ceremonies with which Native society is hampered? Caste says, 'No, you will be excommunicated.'"

There are thousands of educated Hindus who feel these social evils almost as acutely as Mr. M. Malabari, and make speeches against them; but, with a few noble exceptions, they submit to the yoke of caste all the same.

Considering the tyranny of the system, it must be allowed that it requires a considerable amount of moral courage to resist it. Sir Monier Williams gives the following illustration of its working:—

"When I was in Gujarat, in 1875, a man named Lallu-bhai, a cloth merchant of Ahmedabad, was proved to have committed a heinous caste crime. He had married a widow of his own caste, and to marry a widow is, in the eyes of a Hindu, a most awful offence. A woman once married, belongs to one husband for time and eternity. Forthwith, he was sentenced to complete excommunication. No one, either of his own or any other caste, was to be allowed to associate with him; no one was to eat with him; no one was to have any trade dealings with him; no one was to marry any of his children; no temple was to receive him as a worshipper; and if he died, no one was to carry his body to the burning ground. On the morning after the sentence was passed, he went to the bazaar as usual, but not a person would buy from him or sell to him, he could get no home to live in; and none of his debtors would pay him their debts. It was impossible to sue them, as no one would give evidence. He was a ruined man, and had to leave the country, and obtain Government employment in a distant city." *

5. **Individual Liberty is crushed.**—"The caste of India," says Sherring, "is indissolubly blended with the social life of the Hindu,

* *Religious Thought and Life in India*, pp. 472, 473.

and is as much a necessity to him as food to eat, as raiment to wear, and as a house to live in. Indeed, he can often dispense with raiment, and during most of the year he prefers the court outside his house to the hot rooms within; but he can never free himself from caste, can never escape from its influence."

Caste has its "thousand and one" regulations, nearly all childish and frivolous, and some of them leading to much suffering. "Does a Brahman," says the *Indu Prakash*, "wish to dine with a man of another caste? However thick friends they may be of one another, caste says, 'No, you must not do that, or you will be excommunicated.' If a Brahman feel thirsty and has no other water but such as is brought by a Sudra near him, he cannot drink it; for caste forbids it at the pain of excommunication." During famines people, dying of hunger, have refused food offered to them by Europeans.

"An individual Hindu," says Dr. Duff, "follows the example of his caste, just as a sheep or a wild pigeon follows the example of the flock. There are *local* variations observable in the customs and usages of the same caste. In one place a Hindu will consent to do what in another he would peremptorily refuse to do, simply because in the former he is countenanced by the example of his brethren and not in the latter; just as a flock of sheep or pigeons may, from accidental causes, somewhat vary its habits or movements in different localities." There is no true liberty among the Hindus; they are the bondslaves of caste.

6. **The Growth of Nationality is hindered.**—The Hindus love their children, they are zealous for their caste; but except in the case of the enlightened few, their sympathies do not extend beyond these narrow limits. Hence Max Müller says, "The Indian never knew the feeling of nationality"—he did not think of his country *as a whole.*

The Romans had a maxim, "Divide and conquer." The Brahmans acted on the same principle. By splitting up the people into numerous sections, they more easily retained their supremacy. "A nation divided against itself, is the proper description of the Hindu race." Hence they have become an easy prey to foreign invaders. Sir Lepel Griffin, as quoted, thinks it politic on the part of the British Government to encourage caste.

A new feeling of nationality is springing up among educated Indians, but this is in direct opposition to caste. The "National Congresses," regarded with enthusiasm, would be impossible under Manu's caste regulations. Sudras compose the great majority of the population; but if they had presumed to attend and sit in the presence of the "twice-born," banishment and mutilation would have been the reward of their presumption.

7. **Discord between classes.**—This is especially the case in South India, where the hold of caste is strongest. There an

additional division prevails of *Right-hand* and *Left-hand* castes. Dubois thus describes the result :—

"This particular distinction has turned out to be the most baneful that could have been imagined for the tranquillity of the state, and the most injurious to the peace of the citizens It has proved the perpetual fountain of disturbance and insurrections among the people, and a continued principle of endless jealousy and animosity amongst all members of the community

"The opposition between the *Right-hand* and the *Left-hand* arises from certain privileges to which they both lay claim; and where any encroachment is made by either, it is instantly followed by tumults Gentlest of all creatures, timid under all other circumstances, here only the Hindu seems to change his nature There is no danger that he fears to encounter in maintaining what he terms his right, and rather than yield it he is ready to make any sacrifice and even to hazard his life

"I may be permitted to relate one instance at which I myself was present The dispute was between the caste of Pariahs and shoemakers, and produced such dreadful consequences through the whole district where it happened that many of the peaceable inhabitants had begun to leave their villages for a place of greater safety. Fortunately in this instance, matters did not come to an extremity, as the principal inhabitants of the district seasonably came forward to mediate between these vulgar castes, and were just in time, by good management, to disband the armed ranks on both sides that only waited the signal of battle

"One would not easily guess the cause of this dreadful commotion. It arose forsooth from a shoemaker, at a public festival, sticking red flowers in his turban, which the Pariahs insisted that none of his caste had a right to wear."

Dr. Cornish mentions another claim. "The right-hand castes have the privilege of erecting *twelve* pillars to sustain their marriage booths, while the left-hand castes may not have more than *eleven* pillars!

"The quarrels arising out of these small differences of opinion were so frequent and serious in the seventeenth century that in the town of Madras it was found necessary to mark the respective boundaries of the right and left hand castes, and to forbid the right hand castes in their processions from occupying the streets of the left hand, and *vice versâ*."*

With a more efficient police, such open caste disputes are now rare, but the spirit remains. A few years ago a great disturbance was threatened in Masulipatam, because certain castes whitewashed their houses. The magistrate refusing to prevent this, a telegram was sent direct to the Governor.

The Madras Census Report for 1881 says, "Except the members of the admittedly degraded and depressed castes, each Shudra

---

* *Madras Census Report* for 1871, p. 129.

thinks, or professes to think, his caste better than his neighbour's. The Shanar claims to be a Rajput. The Kammala and the Pattnul (weavers) growl that, if they had their rights, they would be recognised as Brahmans."

There are constant quarrels about precedence, nor is it confined to this. The Bengali writer on caste already quoted says:—

> "Each of these divisions (the lower orders) has a class of men called parámániks, members of which exercise the most unlimited inquisitional powers, each within his own jurisdiction of one or more villages, prying even into the minutest circumstances of life, and interfering with every domestic incident, unless bought off with a bribe. Thus domestic happiness, the dearest of all dear things on earth, is subjected to the vulgar intrusion and despotic interference of men who make their inquisitiveness the source of their wealth."

"Instead," says Principal Caird, "of breaking down artificial barriers, waging war with false separations, softening divisions and undermining class hatreds and antipathies, religion becomes itself the very consecration of them"

8. **The Heart is hardened against Suffering.**—A few illustrations of this may be given.

As far as the rules of caste allow, the Hindus are as hospitable as most other nations; but it is a sufficient excuse for not rendering help that the sufferer belongs to a lower class or to a class unknown. Bishop Heber writes:—

> "A traveller falls down sick in the streets of a village, (I am mentioning a fact which happened ten days ago,) nobody knows what caste he is of, therefore nobody goes near him, lest they should become polluted He wastes to death before the eyes of the whole community, unless the jackals take courage from his helpless state to finish him a little sooner, and, perhaps, as happened in the case to which I alluded, the children are allowed to pelt him with stones and mud."

The late Dr. Wilson, of Bombay, says, "I have seen a man lying crushed with broken limbs beneath a cocoa-nut tree which had fallen upon him, while the spectators were making no effort to remove the destructive load from his body."

The above are not solitary cases. The Rev. J. Vaughan says:—

> "Outside their own caste the weal or woe of their fellows affect them in no degree whatever. We have again and again witnessed along the great pilgrim routes of India harrowing illustrations of this sad truth. We have seen poor creatures, smitten with disease, lying on the roadside passed by hundreds of their co-religionists with no more concern than if they were dying dogs; we have seen the poor parched sufferers with folded hands and pleading voice crave a drop of water to moisten their lips, but all in vain Hundreds thus perish, untended, unpitied, unaided; perhaps even before death does its work, the vultures and

jackals begin theirs, and thus lines of whitened bones and blackened skulls, border the roads leading to the sacred shrines, and whence this worse than brutal callousness? What has dried up the springs of human sympathy? *It is Caste.* This first of all taught the people to look upon differing castes as different species; it next taught the lesson of defilement by contact; thus utter isolation and heartless selfishness account for the whole of the sickening scenes described."*

More enlightened views are beginning to prevail among some, and a large-hearted benevolence, embracing all, is not unfrequently exhibited. Still, such is not the caste spirit.

9 **Caste seeks to degrade nearly the whole Human Race, and ranks some beneath the brutes**—The most refined Englishman is an impure Mlechcha When Sir Monier Williams, the Oxford Professor of Sanskrit, first visited India, he was struck by the fact that pandits always came to see him early in the morning. He learned afterwards that it was to save an additional bathing from the pollution they had contracted by meeting him. Even a Sudra has been known to beg a European not to enter his house, to avoid the expense of getting it purified. This would not be required in the case of a dog The very shadow of a European is defiling to a felon in a jail, and will make him throw away his food. The same thing happened when a little English girl, by chance, touched the wooden platform on which two prisoners were preparing food · the whole was thrown away.

According to caste, the great majority of the Hindus are born slaves. Quotations have been given from Manu as to the way in which they are to be treated and regarded. But the height of injustice and cruelty is reached in the case of the Chandals and some other castes (see p. 18.)

Mr. Sherring thus describes the condition of the low castes and the feelings with which they are looked upon :—

"For many long ages they have been a down-trodden and oppressed race, have been treated by the higher castes almost as savages, have been purposely kept ignorant and debased, have been compelled to labour very hard for the scantiest fare, and have been led to regard themselves in the same light in which they are regarded by other castes, namely, as an unclean, vile, ungodly, and contemptible race, not worthy to enter a temple or to come near a Brahman, or to perform any religious duty except vicariously through the priests, or to receive the smallest amount of useful knowledge, or to hold any position except that of serf and clods of the ground."

"The repugnance to the outcaste is hereditary. The Hindus impart it to their children; they hand it down from one generation to another; they display it perpetually in their dealings with this unfortunate race, whom they vilify by the use of every epithet of abuse which can possibly

* *The Trident, the Crescent and the Cross*, pp. 31, 32.

pourtray the loathing and disgust with which their minds are filled. No amount of patient, faithful, and ill-rewarded service, performed by a member of those despised tribes, can soften the heart of the Brahman or Rajput, and lead him to think and act differently.*

Sir Lepel Griffin says, "Much of Central India is inhabited by Bhils, an ancient people of singularly gentle and simple ways. But it is exceedingly difficult to persuade the Rajput chiefs and their Brahman ministers to treat their subject Bhils with common humanity. They look down upon them as dogs, whom only the eccentric philanthropy of the British Government can find excuse for protection."

In Travancore certain castes ought not to come nearer to a Brahman than 74 paces. They are required to make a grunting noise as they pass along, that if necessary on the approach of their superiors, they may retreat from the high road.

The so-called low castes have some of them very disagreeable but necessary duties to perform. Without them, cities would soon become uninhabitable. The feeling towards them should rather be one of gratitude than repugnance. It is thus well described by Carlyle:—

"Venerable to me is the hard hand, crooked, coarse, wherein notwithstanding lies a cunning virtue indefeasibly royal as of the sceptre of this planet. Venerable, too, is the rugged face, all weather-tanned, besoiled, with its rude intelligence, for it is the face of a man living man-like. Oh, but the more venerable for thy rudeness and even because we must pity as well as love thee, hardly-entreated brother! For us was thy back so bent, for us were thy straight limbs and fingers so deformed; thou wert our conscript on whom the lot fell, and fighting our battles, were so marred. For in thee, too, lay a God-created form, but it was not to be unfolded; encrusted must it stand with the thick adhesions and defacements of labour, and thy body, like thy soul, was not to know freedom. Yet, toil on, toil on; *thou* art in thy duty, be out of it who may."

10. **Caste fills a few with pride and arrogance.**—There are proud and haughty men in all countries; but the pride of the Brahmans is peculiar. Their pretensions are thus stated by Dr. Wilson:—

"They only must read and interpret the Vedas. Their wrath is as terrible as that of the gods. They claim to have kicked, beaten, cursed, and frightened, and degraded the highest deities, and distressed and destroyed their children. One of their number, Brihaspati, the instructor of the gods, is said to have turned the moon into a cinder; and another, Vishvakarma, to have cut the sun into twelve pieces; Agastya swallowed up the ocean at three sips, and gave it out salt!"

* *Asiatic Quarterly Review*, Vol. I. pp. 468, 469.

The following syllogism, translated from the Sanskrit, is current over India :—

> " The whole world is under the power of the *gods*,
> The gods are under the power of the *mantras*,
> The *mantras* are under the power of the Brahman,
> The *Brahman* is therefore our God."

According to Manu, the Brahman is not to be put to death for the greatest crimes. Garuda, the bearer of Vishnu, used to eat every creature except Brahmans, who, if swallowed, would have caused an insufferable pain in his stomach Manu says :—

"165 A twice-born man, having merely assaulted a Brahman out of desire to slay him, abides a hundred years in the hell Tamisra.

"166 Having designedly struck him out of anger, even with a straw, for 21 births he is born from sinful wombs." Book IV.

Life, however, must not only be preserved, but rendered comfortable. Land given to a Brahman secures heaven; a red cow, a safe passage across the boiling infernal river Vaitarani; a house, a heavenly palace, an umbrella, freedom from scorching heat; shoes, freedom from pain in walking; feasting of Brahmans, the highest merit. A proper gift to a Brahman on a death-bed will secure heaven to a malefactor.

On the other hand, property *taken* from a Brahman entails the heaviest curse. The *Sri Bhugavat* says, " Whosoever taketh property belonging to Brahmans, whether it was given to them by himself or others, is born as a worm on a dunghill for sixty thousand years."

The masses have thus been led to regard the Brahman's curse as the most appalling calamity, and his blessing as the highest possible good.

Through caste, says Dr. Banerjea, " some are puffed up; others are depressed ALL ARE MORALLY DETERIORATED."

11 **Caste concentrates religion on outward ceremony, and perverts moral feeling.**—What offences are punishable by expulsion from caste? Eating, drinking and marrying contrary to rule. Take the case of the Ahmedabad merchant who suffered so much for marrying a widow of his own caste. Suppose he had become a drunkard, ruined his body by debauchery, been guilty of perjury, theft and murder, all these would not have affected his caste. During the Mutiny, Nana Sahib, at Cawnpore, sent butchers to murder a large number of English women and children: all this did not pollute him; but had he spared a little English girl and drunk a cup of pure water from her hand, he would at once have been expelled.

It is true that caste rules with respect to eating and drinking, are often violated. There are numbers of Hindus in Calcutta who eat the flesh of the cow and get drunk in English hotels, who still retain their caste. But let one visit England to study, and he is excluded. A pundit for 5 Rupees will write a tract ridiculing the Hindu gods, but for 5,000 Rs. he would not take a glass of water from a European. Caste is far more to a Hindu than religion.

The Stomach the seat of Hinduism.—It has been well remarked: "Other religions may be seated in the mind and soul—but the stronghold of Hinduism is the stomach. A Hindu may retain his faith against all argument, and against all violence, but mix a bit of beef in his food, and his religion is gone! Not that he renounces it, but that it repudiates him. Let half a dozen Hindus seize one of their own caste, and forcibly thrust forbidden food down his throat, and that man has ceased to have any rights in this world or the next."

Thus the conscience of the Hindu is perverted, and the true distinctions between right and wrong are so far destroyed. The heaviest caste penalties are inflicted for actions which may even be commendable, as going to England for study. "Under caste" says Dr. Duff, "that is accounted sin which is no sin, and that is no sin which is most heinous in the sight of a holy God."

To observe the rules of his caste is the Hindu ideal—the "Whole Duty of Man."

12. **Caste is founded on a blasphemous Falsehood, and leads to Falsehood.**—According to caste, the Deity is an enormous male, with mouth, hands, thighs, and feet, giving rise to different orders of men endowed with different qualities of good and evil,—of *sattva*, *rajas*, and *tamas* (truth, passion, darkness) as they come from God, and with essentially different laws and institutions. These laws, however frivolous, vexatious, and injurious, it ascribes to God, and in his name demands on their behalf universal obedience. It is, consequently, most impious in its very foundations.

Caste is also maintained by falsehood. The supremacy of the Brahman involves constant lying, either implied or uttered. The same remark applies to many of the other castes. There are comparatively few of the higher castes who really are what they claim to be. Of Southern India the last Madras Census Report says:—

"It may be safely accepted that the mass of the people are not Aryan; that indeed none of them are Aryan, except the Brahmans; possibly not all of these, for there are several classes or subdivisions of Brahmans of more or less hazy origin. All the rest of the so-called Hindus may, if they please, call themselves Shudras, but they are in fact a Dravidian or Turanian or Scythian people who have adopted, in a very highly-developed form, the Aryan caste system, whose germs are found in the four-caste system of Manu.

"Of Kshatriyas and Vaishyas there are probably few, although there are many who claim to belong to these Aryan castes. The *soi disant* (self-called) Kshatriyas are principally the small Rajas and their followers of swordsmen, the Bondilis or Muchias and a few more. Those claiming to be Vaishyas are some of the merchant and trading castes. They are very numerous, and the claim has never been admitted for many of them."

"The Shetti is no longer the only merchant or shopkeeper. On the contrary, the potter and the fisherman turned traders merely add Shetti to their names." pp 103, 104.

Dr. Burnell says, "I know some families in Southern Canara which now claim to be Brahmans, and are called so, but inscriptions show that 500 years ago they were Jains. Much doubt is thrown on the origin of the Gurukkal or Savia priests of the Tamil country, and some wealthy traders in Madura have suddenly set up a claim to be Brahmans."*

There are "manufactured Brahmans" also in the north. Hunter's *Orissa* citis "well-known legends of large bodies of aliens being from time to time incorporated even into the Brahman caste." The same writer says, "In many outlying Provinces, we see non-Aryan chiefs and warlike tribes turn into Aryan Rajputs before our eyes." The Bengali defender of caste in the *Calcutta Review*, says, "Just now there is a hot controversy going on in Hindu society as to whether or not the Bunnya caste in Bengal are the representatives of the ancient Vaisya caste."

It was the same even in early times. Yudishthira says in the Vana-parva: "O most sapient Serpent, birth is difficult to be discriminated in the present condition of humanity, on account of the confusion of all castes. All (sorts of) men are continually begetting children on all (sorts of) women."

The foregoing evils of caste refer to the whole of India; but its worst type is to be found in the Kulinism of Bengal. A king, named Ballala Sen, a son of the river Brahmaputra (!), gave the title of *Kūl* or honourable, to certain Brhmans. Brahmans of a lower order are most anxious to get a Kulin son-in-law. Hence large sums are paid to them to marry their daughters. There are Kulins with twenty, fifty, or even a hundred wives. But the marriage of Kulin females is cruelly stringent, these must not on any account be given to any unless they are of an equal or superior grade. The poor Kulin father is often in the greatest difficulty. He cannot allow his daughter to marry any one of a lower grade; he cannot afford to purchase a husband in his own. It would be a great disgrace to allow her to remain unmarried. His only resource is to appeal to some decrepit old Kulin Brahman, who has already a multitude of wives, to save the honour of his family by adding one more to his list.

Kulin polygamy carries with it a license to indulge, to an almost

* Translation of *The Ordinances of Manu* p. 6

unlimited extent, the vilest passions of human nature, while it occasions an untold amount of misery and crime.*

"The system of caste," says Principal Caird, "involves the worst of all wrongs to humanity—that of hallowing evil by the authority and sanction of religion."

The advantages and disadvantages of caste have now been stated, and the latter are considered far to outweight the former. "Taken in excess even nectar is poison." Sir Lepel Griffin brings forward "contentment" as one of the good results of caste. But "contentment" may be simply a proof of degradation. Bishop Caldwell says of the women of India: "In their own opinion they have nothing to lament as a class, but are as well treated as women could wish to be, and are perfectly content." *The Hindu* says, "The contentment of our people is the result of moral death during centuries."

Granting that the advantages of caste have been greatly underrated, and its disadvantages exaggerated, the retention or abandonment of the system should hinge upon the answer to the following question:

Is caste consistent with strict justice between man and man?

The burning words of Kingsley are true:—

"Foremost among them stands a law which I must insist on, boldly and perpetually, a law which man has been trying in all ages, as now, to deny, or at least to ignore; though he might have seen it if he had willed, working steadily in all times and nations. And that is—that as the fruit of righteousness is wealth and peace, strength and honour; the fruit of unrighteousness is poverty and anarchy, weakness and shame. It is an ancient doctrine and yet one ever young. The Hebrew prophets preached it long ago, in words which are fulfilling themselves around us every day, and which no new discoveries of science will abrogate, because they express the great root-law, which disobeyed, science itself cannot get a hearing."†

As well may men gather grapes from thorns and figs from thistles, as expect good results, on the whole, from an iniquitous system.

Caste is very much like slavery. Under good masters slavery has its advantages; but, taking it all in all, it is to be condemned for its injustice. So with caste. The old Romans had a saying, "Let justice be done though the heavens should fall." This, in the end, is the wisest and best course.

Opinions of Caste.

The writer, in the estimation of the observers of caste and of some of its European advocates, may seem to have painted the

* Abridged from *Modern Hinduism*, by Wilkins.

† Limits of Exact Science applied to History.

disadvantages of caste in too strong colours. Each feature ought to be examined, and its consistency with truth considered. But the view he has given is the same as that held by some of the ablest and most intelligent men in India, deeply interested in the welfare of the country.

A "member of the highest, wealthiest and most influential of the strictest sect of Brahmans," in an Essay on Caste, for the following reasons, pronounces it a "HUGE SHAM" :—

"How many of us, may I ask, satisfy the requirements of caste? I do not mean among our own heterodox selves, but among the bigoted conservatives, who with our uneducated women form the stronghold of the caste ethics? Our motto seems to be, not that they should not be violated, but that we should take care not to be found out in the breach. Ninety-nine out of a hundred Brahmans do not perform the *Sandhya* in proper time, never study the Vedas at all, seldom think of the sacrifices required daily, and do not even wash as often as the rules enjoin. Yet no one objects. We go through the ceremonies in a mechanical way, either without understanding them, or without being edified if we do. We are, without the slightest compunction, reciting the Vedas in the hearing of those who, if Manu were the ruler, would have had molten lead poured into their ears for their pains! We are content even to study our own Vedas from non-Brahmanical pandits like Max Müller. We talk glibly of widow marriages and sea voyages, and shock the orthodox world beyond all forgiveness. We have renounced our ancestral and Gita-prescribed pursuits of life and duties, and have adopted mammon worship in hundreds of ways. We never even make a *namaskára* to our idols, and, like consumate cynics, sneer at the most serious observances of our orthodox brethren. We educate our girls, and make them study our sacred literature in the teeth of tenets which degrade our women to the level of Sudras. What prevents our travelling in other lands and acquiring practical wisdom? What makes our practical religion so ridiculous in the eyes of other religionists? CASTE. It is demoralizing in its effects, engenders self-sufficiency, narrows our sympathies, and is alike oppose to reason and conscience. Its refrain is that the bulk of the human race should for ever hopelessly continue to be the helots of a narrow oligarchy irrespective of religious purity, wealth or intellectual superiority. It in effect represents the Divine Father of mankind as a partial Being, with human and earthly passions and leanings. I repeat therefore that caste is a HUGE SHAM, and if we are true to ourselves, to human nature, to God's eternal laws, and to our country's real good, we ought to renounce it."*

Pandit Shiva Nath Sastri.—The following are the heads of a lecture on the effects of the caste :—

(1) It has produced disunion and discord. (2) It has made honest manual labour contemptible in this country. (3) It has checked internal and external commerce. (4) It has brought on physical degeneracy by

* Quoted in the *Indian Evangelical Review*.

confining marriage within narrow circles. (5) It has been a source of conservatism in every thing (6) It has suppressed the development of individuality and independence of character. (7) It has helped in developing other injurious customs, such as early marriage, the charging of heavy matrimonial fees, &c. (8) It has successfully restrained the growth and development of national worth; whilst allowing opportunity of mental and spiritual culture only to a limited number of privileged people, it has denied these opportunities to the majority of the lower classes, consequently it has made the country negatively a loser. (9) It has made the country fit for foreign slavery by previously enslaving the people by the most abject spiritual tyranny.

Babu Keshab Chandra Sen.—An appeal to "Young India," contains the following :—

"Next to idolatry and vitally connected with its huge system is caste You should deal with it as manfully and unsparingly as with idolatry. That Hindu castism is a frightful social scourge no one can deny. It has completely and hopelessly wrecked social unity, harmony, and happiness, and for centuries it has opposed all social progress. But few seem to think that it is not so much as a social but as a religious institution that it has become the great scourge it really is As a system of absurd social distinctions, it is certainly pernicious But when we view it on moral grounds it appears as a scandal to conscience, and an insult to humanity, and all our moral ideas and sentiments rise to execrate it, and to demand its immediate extermination. Caste is the bulwark of Hindu idolatry and the safeguard of Brahminical priesthood. It is an audacious and sacrilegious violation of God's law of human brotherhood. It makes civil distinctions inviolable divine institutions, and in the name of the Holy God sows perpetual discord and enmity among His children! It exalts one section of the people above the rest, gives the former, under the seal of divine sanction, the monopoly of education, religion and all the advantages of social pre-eminence, and visits them with the arbitrary authority of exercising a tyrannical sway over unfortunate and helpless millions of human souls trampling them under their feet and holding them in a state of miserable servitude. It sets up the Brahminical order as the very vicegerents of the Deity and stamps the mass of the population as a degraded and unclean race, unworthy of manhood and unfit for heaven. Who can tolerate this woeful despotism, this system of abhorrent slavery, this robbery of divine authority? Fellow-countrymen, if you abjure idolatry and rally under the heavenly standard of the true God, you must establish and organize a new brotherhood on the basis of enlightened thoughts and sentiments: in this reformed alliance you must discard and discountenance all caste distinctions, that truth may be freely embraced by all, Brahmin and Sudra alike, and both by virtue of birthright may secure access to the blessings of spiritual freedom, progress and happiness, without let or hindrance. Abandon idolatry and seek the worship of the true God; kill the monster caste and form a rational and religious brotherhood of all your reformed countrymen"

Rev. Dr. Duff.—Educated Hindus, throughout India, owe a deep debt of gratitude to this distinguished missionary. It was largely through his influence that the modern system of education was introduced. What did he think of the effects of caste?

"In point of fact, has not caste, even in the judgment of many of the more candid of its favourers and palliators, *tended*, in all ages, under all changes of dynasty, and amid circumstances the most diverse, to cramp and paralyse the vigour of the mental faculties,—to retard, if not wholly obstruct, the progress of civilization,—to arrest and freeze up the genial current of benevolent feeling, and saturate the whole soul with an isolating, accursed selfishness,—to extinguish every spark of true patriotism, and quench all zeal in the promotion of joint enterprises of public utility, —to banish alike the conception and the reality of human duties and virtues, or duties and virtues pertaining to man as man,—to defeat the ends of truth and righteousness between man and man, and aid and abet the notorious national habits of cruelty and perjury,—to form and consolidate, as by the spell of a freemasonry, those harpy-like fraternities of religious mendicants, and other unproductive classes, that gorge themselves on the very life-blood of the industrious throughout the land,—to facilitate the associated aggregation of dacoits, thugs, and other desperate confederacies for the commission of deadly crimes,—to foster and encourage secret cabals, plots, and conspiracies, that may burst forth in a tempest of conflagration and rapine, massacre and blood,—to externalise all morality, converting it into a ceaseless round of forms, rites and ceremonies, the most puerile, unmeaning, and degrading; thus practically annihilating all moral distinctions, leaving the people without a conscience, and the universe without a God or Righteous Moral Governor?'*

Indu Prakash—Some extracts have already been made from this influential Bombay journal. The remainder is given below:—

"The question is not about going to England, but about an unmanly submission to the vilest and most absurd prejudices of the caste system and Hinduism, which nothing can check and uproot but a spirit of noble independence, rigid moral firmness, and genuine patriotism The prohibition to go to England is the least of our complaints against the tyranny of caste"

It "extends from the most trifling to the most important affairs of Hindu life. It cripples the independent action of individuals, sows the seed of bitter discord between the different sections of society, encourages the most abominable practices, and dries up all the springs of that social, moral, and intellectual freedom which alone can secure greatness, whether to individuals or nations."

"Oh God, have mercy on our fallen-countrymen! Give them true knowledge of Thy Fatherhood, and their brotherhood; that our countless millions may be bound by one social tie, and joining hand with hand, and heart with heart, move onward in the path of freedom and righteousness, knowledge and glory, and national regeneration."

---

* *The Indian Rebellion*, pp. 344—346.

DUTY WITH REGARD TO CASTE.

This is a question of the greatest importance and of no small difficulty. So long as it is confined to talk, its settlement is easy; but practical action is a very different thing.

Some writers dwell upon the evil that would result from the immediate abolition of caste. This is the last thing to be dreaded. Caste will "die hard." The fear is—not lest it should give up the ghost too quickly, but lest it should require to apologize, like Charles II. for being such an "unconscionable time" in taking its departure. In one form or another, it will exist on the earth as long as the human race in its present condition. "The spirit of caste never dies."

Duty with regard to caste may be noticed, in turn, under three heads—the British Government, Hindus, and Christians.

I. Duty of Government.

The British Government should no longer use its vast influence to maintain caste distinctions.—The Sepoy Rebellion was a terrible result of petting and pampering caste. It is granted that something has already been done. Means have been taken to prevent caste combinations in the Native army. All castes may draw water from public wells, be admitted into public schools, and sit together in railway carriages. The fact that Brahmans have had practically a monopoly of Government official service has also received some attention. Dr. Cornish remarked :—

"Politically it is not to the advantage of the Government that every question connected with the progress of the country should be viewed through the medium of Brahman spectacles. The contempt which the Brahmans evince for the lower classes, is in itself a serious bar to their usefulness in many phases of official life, and the true policy of the state would be to limit their numbers in official positions, and to encourage a larger proportion of non-Brahmanical Hindus and Mussulmans to enter official service, so as to allow no special pre-eminence, or great preponderance of any particular caste." Census Report for 1871, p. 197.

To the present time, however, the British Government, not *intentionally* but *indirectly*, is one of the chief agencies for the perpetuation of caste distinctions, and with them of caste feuds. This is done in two ways :—

1. *By registering in the Census Returns the most minute caste distinctions, and entering them in a scale graded according to caste ideas.*—The Madras Census Returns for 1881 gave 19,044 Caste names (Report, vol. I. p. 102). Dr. Cornish says, "The castes are entered in the order in which native authorities are pretty generally agreed as the order of their relative importance." (Report for 1871,

p. 117). The arrangement and the number belonging to each in the Madras Presidency in 1881 are given in the following table :—

No.	Caste Name.	Occupation.	Total Number.
1	Brahmans	Priests	1,122,070
2	Kshatriyas	Warriors	193,550
3	Shetties	Traders	640,047
4	Vellalars	Cultivators	7,767,463
5	Idaiyars	Shepherds	1,586,000
6	Kammalars	Artizans	849,901
7	Kanakkan	Writers	102,472
8	Kaikalar	Weavers	979,062
9	Vanniyan	Labourers	3,751,093
10	Kushavan	Potters	263,975
11	Satani	Mixed Castes	625,455
12	Shembadavan	Fishermen	873,448
13	Shanan	Toddy-drawers	1,621,111
14	Ambattan	Barbers	348,390
15	Vannan	Washermen	528,535
16	Pariahs	Labourers	4,439,253
17	Others, including "Not Stated."	......	2,811,841
			28,497,666

Government, of course, repudiates all claim to settle precedence,—of placing shepherds above writers, fishermen above toddy-drawers, &c., but the effect is all the same. Shepherds, in the Government Tables, are of the fifth grade; writers of the seventh, &c. Such a classification may gratify the pride of a small section, but it tends to perpetuate caste disputes among the great bulk of the population.

It should be stated that in the Census Returns Native Christians are not required to give their original castes.

2. *By entering Caste Distinctions in other public documents and making inquiries in Court about Caste.*

The Bombay Government Education Directory* may be given as an example. It contains a column, "Caste or Religion." The following are some of the entries. "Vania, Brahman, Hindu, Kshatriya, Bania, Coppersmith, Kunbi, Lohar, Mali, &c."

With regard to the other point, the following illustrations may be given. In the Telugu country, to the north of Madras, numbers belonging to the shoemaker caste, considered one of the most degraded, have become Christians. Brahman officials, when summoning them as witnesses, &c., have wished to add to their Christian names the opprobrious caste designation. English Magistrates in

* *See Bombay Educational Record* for April, 1887.

Court have tried to elicit it from the witnesses themselves. The attempt, in some cases, has been successfully resisted. A witness, when asked to give his caste, has simply said, "I am a Christian," and the Magistrate has been obliged to give way. If a Hindu is thrust out of his caste by becoming a Christian, there is no justice in compelling him to answer to the caste name.

No part of the Proclamation of 1858 is more frequently quoted than

"It is our further will, that, so far as may be, our subjects, of whatever race or creed, be freely and impartially admitted to offices in our service, the duties of which they may be qualified by their education, ability and integrity, duly to discharge."

Brahmans and other so-called high castes consider the employment of a comparative handful of Europeans as a breach of this pledge; but they think it quite proper to exclude the lower castes.

The following recommendations by the late Dr. Duff indicate the right course on the part of Government:—

"Let us henceforth proclaim it to all India and the world, that in future, we are, as a Government, to have nothing whatever to do with caste, as such,—that we are to ask no questions concerning it—that we are to look to the *highest qualifications* for particular business in view, and to *these alone*, as the determining elements in the selection of candidates. Let us honestly act out the spirit and intent of such a proclamation, by practically proving to India and the world, that whosoever brings the most eminent qualifications into the labour-market throughout every department—military, judicial, fiscal, police, or educational—must thereby ensure a decided preference, and fetch the highest price. And let it further be made to be felt, that mental attainments, original and acquired, as well as official aptitude, actual or potential, being equal, he will be the object of choice whose moral character, not in the Hindu ceremonial sense, but in the true European or Christian sense, is best established; or whose openly avowed and consistently professed moral and religious principles may furnish the surest guarantee for uprightness and conscientiousness in the discharge of duty.

"In actually carrying out such an ordinance, let it be decreed that in *registering* the names of successful candidates, their *proper names alone*, and not, most as frequently hitherto, *their caste* be *officially recorded*; or if, in addition to the bare name, there be columns for place of nativity, seminary of education, or any other item of identification, let it still be *peremptorily forbidden to have any separate column for caste.*

"In these several ways, let caste, without any violent or forcible interference, be simply and absolutely ignored by our Christian Government in connexion with the hundreds of thousands of offices at its disposal throughout every branch of the public service, and the effect will, in time, be found vastly to exceed the apparent smallness and simplicity of the means. The mere fact of such universal and continuous non-recognition of caste by the paramount and sovereign power will silently operate on the Asiatic mind as by a slow but a steady process of attrition; and, along with other and more potent influences, will eventually succeed in reducing its once lofty and proud pretensions into something like a fluent, or constantly diminishing and finally evanescent, quantity

"Besides its simplicity and practicability, the grand advantage of adopting such a course is, that it obviously involves no violence to religious scruples,—no restraint on liberty of conscience."*

Mr. Sherring, in his elaborate work on Caste, makes similar recommendations :—

"In regard to not a few situations of importance under the Government, the question is at once asked of candidates, 'To what caste do you belong?' Official notices commonly state the castes of Government servants; and thus those of low caste, although holding, it may be, as good positions as those of higher castes, are held up to obloquy and contempt. I believe this is altogether unintentional on the part of the Government. Nevertheless, it is beyond dispute that caste is invigorated, and honoured, by the public attention which is thus paid to it. Moreover, Hindus of good caste, naturally feel that they stand in favour with the Government, by virtue of their caste, and in proportion to its rank, to the disadvantage of Hindus of lower castes, who, on the other hand, are painfully conscious of the comparative dishonour with which they are regarded, and treated, on account of caste inferiority. So inveterate is the habit, in some Government departments, of stating in official documents, the castes of Hindu employees, that even when a Hindu becomes a Christian he is still compelled to state his caste, which, in his case, is the Christian *caste*. This recognition of caste by the British Government in India is a custom which it most likely inherited when it took possession of the country and which it has unwittingly observed to the present time, for it would be unjust, as well as absurd, to imagine that the Government, which has so determinately severed itself from all connexion with the Hindu idolatry, would knowingly lend its influence to the propping up of Hindu caste Still it has done so. Henceforward, however, its connexion with it should cease It should not recognize the institution in any way whatever. Its official documents, its monthly forms, pay bills, and other papers containing descriptions of its servants, should make no allusion to it Specially, should the question never be asked of a candidate for a post under Government what is your caste? The candidate's suitability for a post should be decided by his qualifications, altogether apart from the subject of caste.' In short, the Government should carefully abstain by fitting regulations from sanctioning such an obnoxious and terrible social evil."†

Mr. Sherring urges the same course upon merchants and private employers of labour that he does upon Government.

---

* *The Indian Rebellion*, pp 350-352.

† Quoted in *Indian Evangelical Review*, Vol. VII. pp. 191-192.

To the foregoing may be added the opinion of Sir John Lawrence, in a Punjab order during the Mutiny :—

"The system of caste can no longer be permitted to *rule* our services Soldiers and Government servants of every class must be entertained for their merits, irrespective of creed, caste or class

The great argument for the retention of caste names is for identification. It may be asked how is this secured in all other countries of the world where caste does not exist? The three following entries are sufficient

1. *The name.*—If a person choose to retain in his name the caste section to which he belongs, as Banerjea, Mudaliar, &c, to this there is no objection. When a claim hinges upon belonging to a particular caste, the question may be put. It is a *separate general heading for caste* that is condemned.

2. *Employment.*

3. *Place of Residence.*

These are enough for postal purposes and they should suffice in other cases.

It is granted that for statistical objects Caste Returns in the Census Reports are interesting and useful. One great objection might also be obviated by ranking them *alphabetically.* The last Madras Census Report says.—

"Of late years castes have been so infinitely multiplied that, even if there were any recognised principle of precedence, the *nuances* of rank would be so light, that the places of the several castes could not be distinguished.... The test of social pre-eminence, as a guide to grading the castes, is not only an impracticable one, but it will become more so, every year." Report, p. 105.

Still, the disadvantages greatly preponderate even against an alphabetical arrangement. Besides, the great divisions are now sufficiently known. How long the British Government will continue to countenance an unjust system, and help to perpetuate discord among those under its rule, it is hard to say. Great bodies are slow to move. Years of agitation were needed before British troops in India were released from firing salutes in honour of idols. The Bishop of Madras was even censured by the Madras Government for proposing its discontinuance. The British Government long employed Brahmans to pray for rain, while the Ceylon Government paid for "devil dances" for "Her Majesty's Service."

Some members of Government, like Sir Lepel Griffin, think caste useful in preventing rebellion. Even politically, however, it has its disadvantages. It is sometimes used for combinations to conceal injustice and crime. The terrorism and "boycotting" of the National League, which the British Government is trying to suppress in Ireland, is simply a reproduction of the Indian caste ban. The case of the Ahmedabad merchant has been noticed at page 25.

Not a few European officers become Brahmanised through the influence of their caste subordinates. This has caused the most public-spirited Native of Ceylon, who has made the largest contributions for the benefit of the Island, to be passed over in the distribution of Jubilee honours, to please a selfish class, who have sought only their own advancement, and the degradation of large bodies of their countrymen

The words of Kingsly have already been quoted. The throne is not to be established by iniquity. Justice between man and man is the only secure basis of Government, and every other foundation is rotten.

Dr Burnell justly characterises the "Introduction on Caste," in the Madras Census Report of Dr. Cornish, as "invaluable." Few Europeans had better opportunities for examining the working of caste. His opinion is not that of a Missionary or an "irresponsible pamphleteer," but of a public officer without bias, after careful investigation. The Introduction concludes with the words that caste "is now the greatest bar to the advance of the Indian people in civilization and aptitude for self-government." Report, p. 130.

The writer strongly disowns any desire to deal unfairly with Brahmans. So long as they are the best qualified candidates for office, let them be appointed. From their superior advantages for unnumbered generations, they are long likely to retain their superiority. On the other hand, they should not have any preference simply on the ground of their caste "A fair field and no favour," should be the guiding principle. There is a Latin proverb, *detur digniori*, "Let it be given to the more worthy." As Lord Kenyon, a Chief Justice of England, remarked, "There is no rule better established respecting the disposal of every office, in which the public are concerned than this."

It may be urged that the object of Government is rather to discourage caste by a column for it in the Returns—it is intended to guard against a preponderance of Brahmans. If so, it is not the first case in which we have intensified an evil by our ill-considered remedies.

All that Government is asked to do with regard to caste as suggested by Dr. Duff is, "*simply to ignore its existence altogether.*" He adds:—

"Let there be no direct or violent attack, by the arm of secular power, on it or any of its usages. So long as our native fellow-subjects are in darkness, and know and feel, and believe no better, let them retain and freely practise what usages and customs they please, so far as these do not interfere with the peace and order of society, or openly trench on the grand fundamental laws of general morality. But, while we would studiously abstain from all forcible or sinister means of inducing or compelling them to tear asunder and cast away the encumbering fetters of caste, let us be scrupulously careful, both in word and deed, to refrain from aught that would confound bare tolerance with favouring approbation—simple liberty of conscience with formal sanction of law."*

II. The Duty of Hindus.

1. **It should be made as widely known as possible that caste is not recognised in the Vedas.**

Professor Max Müller first printed the whole of the Rig Veda with the commentary of Sayana; and he has devoted nearly his entire life to its study under the most favourable circumstances. What does he say?

"There is no authority whatever in the hymns of the Veda for the complicated system of castes. There is no law to prohibit the different classes of the people from living together, from eating and drinking together; no law to prohibit the marriage of people belonging to different castes; no law to brand the offspring of such marriages with an indelible stigma. There is no law to sanction the blasphemous pretensions of a priesthood to divine honours, or the degradation of any human being to a state below the animal." *Chips.* Vol. 11.

Mr. J. Siromani, M.A., B.L., and of the College of Pundits, Nadiya, in his *Commentary on Hindu Law*, quotes the following from Goldstücker, a distinguished Sanskrit scholar:—

"The institution of caste, however, seems at the time (the Sanhita period) to have been unknown, for there is no evidence to prove that the names which at a later period were current for the distinction of caste, were employed in the same sense by the poets of these hymns." p. 13.

Mr. Siromani says, "In former times a girl of the lower caste could be taken in marriage. But intermarriage between the several castes is forbidden in the present age. There is no express prohibition in the Shastras as to intermarriage between several classes of the same caste." p. 68.

Mr. K. K. Bhattacharjya, late Professor of Sanskrit in the Presidency College, Calcutta, and Tagore Professor of Law, says, "There is overwhelming evidence in ancient texts that in these days intermarriage among the different castes was of very frequent occurrence."†

The present stringent rules are simply based on custom.

2. **The effects of caste should be carefully considered, and it**

* *The Indian Rebellion*, p. 439.

† *Tagore Law Lectures*, p. 73.

should especially be inquired whether it is consistent with truth and justice.

Not very long ago there were millions of Negro slaves in the West Indies and the United States, owned by Englishmen and Americans. It was most difficult to convince these slaveholders that it was wrong to retain their fellowmen in bondage, to buy and sell them like cattle. It will be as hard a task for those who have all their lives been accustomed to caste to form a dispassionate judgment with regard to its merits. As in the case of the slaveholders also, there is the sacrifice involved if it is wrong. We are easily convinced of what we wish to believe. Still, the duty is plain. God has given us reason, and we are not to act simply like sheep. Our responsibility is the same although we seek to evade it.

3. **If caste is founded on a blasphemous falsehood and is unjust, it should be felt to be sinful to countenance it in any way.—**

The late Rev. Dr. Krishna Mohun Banerjea says ·

" Such of our readers as have not absolutely surrendered their mental freedom to the pretended authority of the Vedas and Puranas, should consider the guilt of conforming to a system which is falsely attributed to a divine original Of all forgeries the most flagitious and profane is that, which connects the name of the Almighty with an untruth. If the Brahman, the Kshatriya, the Vaishya, and the Sudra did not really proceed from different parts of the Creator's person, the story is nothing short of blasphemy He who professes assent to such a story by his conformity to the institution of caste is *particeps criminis* (a sharer in the crime) Even if it were abstractedly right to classify a people, it would still be a participation in the spiritual forgeries of the Shastras to support the specific institution which they have originated."

It must be acknowledged that an enlightened conscience is needed for this feeling. Hindus are familiar with stories of their highest gods, charging them with the most heinous crimes. Brahma, the fabled Creator, is said to have been cursed for his evil deeds, and deprived of worship Accustomed from infancy to the observance of caste, it becomes a kind of second nature. But though conscience has been deadened and perverted, it has not been altogether destroyed. It is difficult to see how any educated man can honestly say that the caste system, as laid down by Manu, is just and righteous. If, on the other hand, it is unjust and unrighteous, its support, in any way, is to be condemned. Sin sits lightly upon the conscience of the Hindu, and to argue that because a thing is wrong in itself he ought to give it up, he regards as a *non sequitur*—not a necessary deduction. It ought to be shown that it is contrary to custom. In time, however, more correct views will prevail.

4. **The Fatherhood of God and the Brotherhood of Man should be recognised and acted upon.**—An English poet says,

> " Children we are all
> Of one Great Father, in whatever clime
> His providence hath cast the seed of life;
> All tongues, all colours "

The Mahabharata has the following:—

> " Small souls inquire 'Belongs this man
> To our own race, or class, or clan?'
> But larger-hearted men embrace
> As brothers all the human race."

That there is no real distinction between men is admitted by all who have any claim to intelligence.

In one of the Pitakas, the sacred books of the Buddhists, it is said, that "Caste is a sound, and nothing but a sound." Ashwagosha argues that different animals can be distinguished by different structure. We can say "this is a bull's foot; that a deer's foot," and so on. But there are no similiar differences between the castes into which men are divided.

Yudhisthira says in the Vana-parva:—

" The speech, the mode of propagation, the birth, the death of all mankind are alike....I have already declared that he is a Brahman in whom purity of conduct is recognised."

The Santi-parva is even more explicit. Bharadvaja says:—

" Desire, anger, fear, cupidity, grief, apprehension, hunger, fatigue, prevail over us all; by what then is caste discriminated? Sweat, urine, excrement, phlegm, bile and blood (are common to all); the bodies of all decay; by what then is caste discriminated? Brigu replies· There is no difference of castes; this world, having been at first created by Brahma entirely Brahmanic, became (afterwards) separated into castes in consequence of works "

"There is a monotheism," says Max Müller, "which precedes the polytheism of the Veda." As already mentioned, the ancestors of the Hindus, Greeks, Romans, and English, once lived together worshipping the same God, under the same name—a name which meant Heaven-Father. The long separated Aryan nations should use again, "the primeval prayer, in that form which will endure for ever, 'Our Father which art in heaven.'"

The Bible says that God "hath made of one blood all nations of men to dwell on all the face of the earth." "Have we not all one father? hath not one God created us?" Let us acknowledge each other as brethren, and treat each other as brethren.

The golden rule should be followed "All things whatsoever ye would that men should do to you, do ye even so to them " This strikes at the root of caste.

5. **No opprobrious caste names should be used, and all should be addressed without indignity.**—It has been shown that there is no such thing as caste distinctions, and that to maintain them is to maintain a falsehood It has also been pointed out that the so-called low castes are very necessary members of the community, and that they are entitled to gratitude rather than disdain on account of the disagreeable duties they have to perform. A Chandal who supports himself and his family by honest labour deserves far more respect than a Brahman who spends his time in idleness and gains his living by false claims. One of the Shastras contains the following: "Caste is not regarded by the gods, but rather those virtues that promote universal happiness: and even an outcaste, if he possesses them, is owned by *them* as a Brahman."

The rudeness of some Europeans is a frequent and, in some cases, a just complaint in Native papers. None regret it more than some of their own countrymen. But there is a religious silence regarding the degradation to which many millions are daily subjected. The *Indian Mirror* justly remarks:

If ten Englishmen behave haughtily towards the Natives, they deserve to be condemned, and they will be condemned throughout the civilised world by every right-thinking man. What we contend for is that while we are apt to animadvert on the overbearing conduct of a certain class of Englishmen, we seem indifferent or perhaps blind to the same defect in ourselves."

The *Times of India* says, "No Englishman treats the Natives of this country with the contempt and insolence which high caste Hindoos habitually display towards their low-caste brethren."

The Sinhalese are said to have 16 forms of the second personal pronoun, ranging from the highest respect to the utmost contempt. The last is constantly used by many of the so-called high castes in speaking to numbers of their fellow-countrymen, rendering to them useful service.

Smiles says, "There are many tests by which a gentleman may be known; but there is one that never fails—how does he *exercise power* over those subordinate to him?" There are men that cringe to their superiors, who, in speaking to their inferiors, could not assume harsher and more contemptuous language were they speaking to a dog.

The last words uttered by the Duke of Wellington were, "Yes, if you please," addressed to a servant who asked him if he would take a cup of tea. The "Great Duke" had been accustomed to command large armies, and to be waited on by some of the noblest in the land; but thus he spoke to one of his common servants.

The Bible command is "Honour all men." Let every person be addressed in terms which do not imply any disrespect.

6. **Subdivisions of the same caste should freely eat together and intermarry.**—It is not desirable, as a rule, for persons widely dissimilar in social position and tastes to marry. A Pariah girl, well educated in a Mission Boarding School, may herself be a suitable match for an educated Brahman, but in India when a man marries a wife he is considered also to marry all her relations, who think they have a right to come and quarter themselves upon him. The first and easiest step is that proposed by Professor Ranganatha Mudaliyar:—

"Can nothing be done to bring into intermarrying relations all the members of a class like Mudaliars or Nayadus? That the son of one Nayadu should marry the daughter of another Nayadu does not seem to involve any violation of the Vedic or Smrithic precepts. No religious scruples need be set at rest, and I presume there will be no great opposition from the priest. Custom is the only foe to contend with. I would fain think that if a small beginning were made in the way of uniting three or four of the many sections of Mudaliyars, the advantageous character of the union would be readily and fully appreciated, and the way be prepared for a further blending together of the sections that now stand apart. In a matter like this, the chief city should set the example, and the towns in the mofussil will follow suit, sooner or later."

It has been shown that the Vedas do not contain any restriction whatever about marriages, and that even in the time of Manu there were intermarriages between the different castes. The present system of forbidding marriages between numerous sections of the same caste is modern, and rests wholly on custom.

7. **Educated men of the same social standing should eat together and their families should intermarry.**—This would be the second step in advance.

The great caste rod of terror is the prohibition of marriage, Hindus feel bound to marry their children, and if outcasted this is impossible according to their ideas. There are now so many educated and intelligent Hindus in the great cities of India, that they outnumber several of the subdivisions that confine intermarriage to themselves. A greater choice of marriage would thus be permitted, while there would also be a greater similarity of tastes and greater happiness. Early marriage would not be necessary, and girls might be properly educated.

It has been proposed that a union of this kind should be formed among educated men, who would bind themselves to intermarry their children. If this were done, it would give a great impulse to the movement throughout India.

8. **Educated men, on returning from Europe, should refuse to make expiation.**—One of the most degrading features of Hinduism is its *animal worship*. No doubt this has existed in all ages among

savage or semi-civilized nations; but perhaps its lowest depth is reached in India. Not only is the cow worshipped, but her very excrements are considered sacred. Her urine is the best of all holy waters—a sin-destroying liquid which purifies every thing it touches. Among the Parsis, it is brought to the house every morning. Cow-dung is supposed to be of equal efficacy. The ashes produced by burning this substance are of such a holy nature that they have only to be sprinkled over a sinner to convert him into a saint.* To swallow a pill composed of the five† products of the cow will even purify a man from the deep pollution of a visit to England.

That the ignorant should cling to caste, is only what might be expected; but it is humiliating that some men who ought to be the leaders of enlightened public opinion bend their necks to its yoke.

Mr. Sherring says of some: "With all their weight of learning the possession of which enables them to carry off University degrees and honours, they are perfectly content to mingle among the most superstitious and ignorant Hindus, to do as they do, to obey their foolish *dictum* as law, and to have no other aim in life than to conform to the most rigid usages of their ancestors."

The *Hindu Patriot*, the leading Native paper, while under the editorship of the late Hon. Kristo Das Pal, remarked:—

"As Indians, we should feel humiliated to see any one of our fellow-Indians, with silly caste-notions in his head, travelling to Europe—especially, when the traveller pretends to represent the rising and educated classes of this great continent. We do not wish people in England, in Europe, to believe that what we call 'education' has not yet freed our intellects from the trammels of superstition; that we are afraid even to drink a glass of pure water from the hands of an Englishman, lest the recording angel should make a damning entry against us in his books! India can never be regenerated till she has outlived the oppressive institution of caste; and she can never outlive the oppressive system of caste, if we are to look to men like . . . . . . who begins like a daring rebel, but ends into an imbecile swallower of penitential pills!"

Mr. N. G. Chandavarker, the Bombay delegate to England, said with truth recently: "Above all, we are a caste-ridden people, and where caste exists, there the political spirit can and will never prosper." Professor Bhandarkar says: "The caste system is at the root of the political slavery of India."

But such disgraceful concessions to caste and animal worship have a far more important bearing than even upon political advancement. Referring to an instance in 1886, The *Indian Messenger* justly remarks:

"We find in this only cause to mourn for we look upon it as one more

* Sir Monier Williams, *Religious Thought in India*, p. 318.

† Milk, curds, ghee, urine, and dung.

act, tending to make the present Hindu society hollow and hypocritical. Under the influence of Western education a young man may discard many things, but let him not discard sincerity, the only thing that can entitle a man to the respect of his fellowmen, and without which no man or no nation was ever ennobled."

All Indians, however, on their return from England, have not acted the part of the poltroon. One good result has been that it is beginning to be admitted that expiation is not necessary.

III THE DUTY OF CHRISTIANS

Professing Christians are especially bound not to exhibit the caste spirit in any degree.—The Hindu thinks that caste has religious authority, and that it is his duty to observe it. The Christian, on the other hand, who keeps caste, is acting in direct opposition to his professed Master. The second great commandment is, "Thou shalt love thy neighbour as thyself" Christ also says, "Ye are brethren." Another precept of the New Testament is, "In honour preferring one another." All these are incompatible with the caste spirit.

Just as the fiercest caste disputes are among Pariahs and shoemakers, so some of the Native Christians who are most tenacious about caste were originally of what are called the lower castes. Brahman converts to Christianity, in general, are more free from the spirit.

The excuse is made that caste is observed among Christians simply as a distinction of rank; but its features and results are the same as in the Hindu system It depends upon birth alone, and is unchangeable. It is founded on pride and falsehood. Its father is Satan, whose condemnation was pride, and who was a liar from the beginning Those who manifest it show by their spirit to whom they belong.

It is not proposed that all classes of Christians should eat together or intermarry. Their tastes and circumstances differ greatly, and, as it as already been remarked with reference to Hindus, dissimilarity in these respects is a bar to happiness in the married life. But in church there should not be any distinction, nor should it once be named among Christians in ordinary life.

Although the Ceylon Buddhists observe caste, it is also contrary to their religion.

PROSPECTS OF CASTE

The motto on the title page, from Sir Madhava Row, applies especially to caste.—

"The longer one lives, observes and thinks, the more deeply does he feel there is no community on the face of the earth which suffers

less from political evils and more from self-inflicted or self-accepted, or self-created, and, therefore, avoidable evils, than the Hindu community ! !"

There is a Persian proverb, "The proper devil of mankind is man." People are their own worst enemies God said, through Jeremiah, of the Jews in ancient times, "The prophets prophesy falsely, and the priests bear rule by their means, and my people love to have it so." The iron of slavery has entered into a soul of the Hindus. They have become "hereditary bondsmen,"—nay, they even hug their fetters. Like ignorant Hindu women, they are quite content, or rather, like the ancient Jews, they "love to have it so." To be unconscious of their degradation is their deepest degradation

The discouragements and encouragements in the way of reform will now be noticed.

Opposition to Reform from False Patriotism.—It has been remarked that the "spirit of caste never dies" At present among a section of educated Hindus it takes the shape of an exaggerated idea of their ancient civilization, and in proof of this they maintain the superiority of their social customs to the changes which certain reformers seek to introduce.

Fifty years ago the words of Burns were hailed with enthusiasm by a large meeting in Calcutta :—

"For a' that, and a' that,
It's comin' yet for a' that,
That man to man, the world o'er
Shall brothers be, for a' that."

The following quotation from the *Indu Prakash* shows a very different spirit :

"The *Indian Messenger* is responsible for the following statement : — 'It was but the other day that we heard of a student of a low caste, who has passed the F. A examination this year, being looked upon with extreme dislike by his fellow-students, who wished that he should not be allowed to sit on the same bench with them' But for the fact that the statement is made by a paper, which is scrupulously accurate in its facts, we should have doubted it. But the fact is—and no one that reads the signs of the times can fail to notice it and be painfully impressed by it—well, we say the fact is that there seems to be a strong, blind, unreasonable, and suicidal reaction in favour of customs which have contributed to the downfall of the ancient Hindu race Caste is good; infant marriage is good enforced widowhood is good."

The *Subodh Patrika* contains the following account of a meeting lately held in Calcutta :—

"The anti-reform spirit which we find displayed in Bombay and Poona among our young graduates and still younger undergraduates and other students has its exact counterpart in Calcutta. At a recent meeting of a students' association in Calcutta, we learn from a Calcutta paper, the subject of early marriages was brought up for discussion One of the speakers had the hardihood to denounce the custom in very strong language. For this he was hissed and laughed at by the audience, nay, such was the feeling displayed at the meeting and such the noise and din which ensued, that the President of the meeting, no less a person than Babu S. N. Banerji, had, we learn, to adjourn the debate to another day. On this occasion, the audience patiently listened to a stout defence of the time-honoured custom, but compelled another speaker who raised his voice against it to resume his seat without completing his speech Thereupon Mr. Banerji called upon Pandit Shivnath Shastri to address the meeting, but he very wisely declined the honour. In this way, did the rising hope of Calcutta establish its patriotism on the occasion "*

Principal Wordsworth, acknowledged to be one of the warmest friends of India, and from his position having the best means of ascertaining the truth, makes the following severe remarks regarding the action of some educated Hindus :—

"I need hardly say, that I consider the existence of the Hindu child-widow one of the darkest blots that ever defaced the civilisation of any people, and it is the direct and necessary consequence of the system of infant marriage. Some years ago I should have expected that these sentiments would have found an echo in the bosom of every Hindu who had received an English education, and particularly among those persons who were attempting to appropriate the political methods and ideas of Englishmen. I have no such delusion now. I find some of them employing all the resources of theological sophistry and cant, not simply to palliate, but to vindicate what is plainly one of the most cruel, blighting, and selfish forms of human superstition and tyranny. I find others manœuvring to arrest every sincere effort at reform, sophisticating between right and wrong, defaming the character and motives of reformers, and labouring to establish by arguments as ridiculous as they are insulting, that English domestic society offers a warning rather than an example to Hindus. I find them vindicating early marriage as the only safeguard against universal sexual license, a confession of moral incompetence which I should have thought that any people with a grain of self-respect would have shrunk from advancing."†

The Hindu complains of somewhat the same spirit being manifested in Madras :—

"We have observed of late a tendency on the part of some of our educated countrymen to apply their mental powers for irrationally reactionary purposes. Social customs and institutions which are evil in their results, and are the product of past simpler and less civilized conditions, have received elaborate defence, and even certain merits

* Quoted in *Bombay Guardian*, 6th August, 1887.
† Letter to Mr. M. Malabari.

have been attached to them. The general community of educated natives have rejected them, if not all of them in practice, but at least in their beliefs, as injurious to social progress, and as being inconsistent with modern civilization Yet we have seen tolerably educated men setting up elaborate defences of them and even going the length of denouncing the majority, not agreeing with them as unpatriotic, denationalized and so forth . . . A sentiment of pride in our own annals is necessary for any people to feel self-respect It is reasonable and wholesome if we indulge it as a stimulus to our attachment to the country and to patriotic reform. But to take a past state of things which is separated from the present by centuries of barbarous history, as the pattern of reform, is to aim not at progression but at retrogression"

The *Indian Messenger* points out the injurious effects upon the moral character, of those who take part in such movements, and attributes them to a false patriotism :—

"We sincerely regret the recent agitation in favour of infant-marriage, not because we are in any way afraid lest it should obstruct the cause of social progress in this country, but because this retrograde movement will tell seriously upon the intellectual honesty of the rising generation, and give a premium to hypocrisy and false self-satisfaction. Infant-marriage is doomed, its utter banishment from society is simply a question of time. We harbour no fear on that score. But the only thing that we regret in connection with the recent agitation is its hollow, insincere character. When people who would never think of giving their own daughters in marriage before they were fully grown up,—who have, in their own family, given practical proofs of their partiality for adult-marriages,—when they now come forward as apologists for early marriages, the value of their agitation may well be ascertained. Most men feel infant-marriage to be a grave social evil—but a false patriotism and a false idea of nationality come in, and kick up a spurious, hollow, and insincere agitation in support of it. That is the real evil. This tendency to hide our own shortcomings, and parade the virtues of social institutions which in our heart of hearts we detest,—this hypocrisy and insincerity—is what we regret most."

Great indignation was expressed at Sir Lepel Griffin on account of the following remarks.—

"The real friends of India are not those who persuade the natives that they are already the equals of their teachers, and that after a few years of imperfect training they are ripe for institutions which, in England, are the outcome of the constitutional struggles of centuries, and have been bought by blood and tears, by much suffering and by long endurance. Let the young Hindu students, who so loudly talk of their grievances, remember that more personal and political freedom is enjoyed by natives of India than is the lot of any modern people in Europe, and that the English nation has no wish to arbitrarily withhold from them any of the rights and privileges of a common citizenship. Let them prove their civilization by emancipating their women from the curse of infant-marriage and virgin widowhood, and admit them to an honoured place, side by side with men let them demonstrate their intellectual power by original research, and their fitness for political enfranchisement by moderation, dignity, and self-restraint; while they refrain from childish abuse of those who tell them that they must learn to walk before they can run. When they have accomplished this, Englishmen will listen with patience to their demand for representative institutions, if by that time they have not become too wise to hanker after so doubtful a blessing."

Some Indian reformers now seem almost inclined to agree with Sir Lepel Griffin. The *Indian Spectator* (10th July, 1887) has the following :—

" In the course of an excellent article, headed, The Cry for Representative Government, last week's *Indu Prakash* makes the following remarks. We have given expression to similar views more than once and hold to these views with greater tenacity the more we see of the work of our 'national representatives' in India. We are led to ask at such moment —*who* are our representatives and *whom* do they represent? These are the reflections of the *Indu Prakash* :—

" We have begun to doubt whether the cause of social reform—where it requires legitimate legislative help—will be promoted if the elective principle be introduced into our Councils just at present. We need more assurance on the point and we are afraid that assurance events that have transpired so far and the spirit that seems to prevail have failed to give us. What will be the gain to the country if men who are sent as its representatives would abolish the Widow Marriage Act or insist on imprisoning women to enforce harsh customs, or if those who would exhibit such a reactionary spirit are returned to the Council? The present attitude towards social reform questions must change, or else it may prove a leap in the dark. Let us not be misunderstood. We fully believe that the life of the country depends on its social arrangements and, therefore, social reform, to our mind, must proceed along, if not precede, political progress Yet we do not mean that changes should be forced on an unwilling people by penal or coercive enactments. What, however, is clearly essential to the success of the cry now so generally raised is that there should be guarantee that the elective legislature will not be actuated by a spirit of blind and caste-ridden conservatism, and that the social problem will meet with a fair treatment, free from the spirit of tyranny which Professor Wordsworth has justly characterised as blighting and selfish."

Some years ago Mr. Manomohun Ghose said :

" He felt a legitimate pride in the ancient civilization of India, but he was bound to say that an undue and exaggerated veneration for the past was doing a great deal of mischief. It was quite sickening to hear the remark made at almost every public meeting that the ancient civilization of India was superior far to that which Europe ever had."

National conceit, instead of being a proof of enlightenment, is exactly the reverse. In vanity the negroes of the Hayti Republic exceed even "Young Bengal." The following illustration is from *Chambers's Journal* —

"The Haytians are an intensely vain people, and the thing they most pride themselves on is their army. Nothing will convince them that as a military power they are not vastly superior to any nation either in the Old or New World. Even those who have lived in European capitals are addicted to this extremely ridiculous 'balderdash;' but when the real facts are presented, the state of affairs disclosed is simply sublime in its absurdity. The Haytian army must present to European beholders a spectacle of grotesqueness, the equal of which it would be difficult to find anywhere either in fact or fiction. Imagine a battalion on parade consisting of thirteen privates, ten officers, and six drummers!—the rest of the men—as the author quaintly puts it—thinking it unnecessary to present themselves except on pay-day. The staff-officers are clad in the most gorgeous uniforms procurable, while the men are habited in a motley array of tatters. Some have coats wanting one arm, the collar, or the tail, the headgear may consist of a dilapidated shako, a straw-hat, wide-awake, or in many cases merely a handkerchief tied round the head. The officers hold their swords in either hand as suits them; and the men march past in admirable confusion, each one carrying his musket in the position he finds most convenient The populace look on with admiring looks, and gravely ask if finer troops can anywhere be found." May, 1887.

The meeting in Calcutta in favour of early marriages that would not allow the opposite side even to be heard, was composed largely of school-boys; but it must be admitted that even many graduates have only a thin whitewash of Western enlightenment—the pure Hindu is immediately below the surface, or, as Mr. Cotton expresses it in *New India*, "Collegiate impressions are at present like a tinselled outdoor decoration, discarded by their possessor as a superfluity in private." (p. 147).

While the English occupy a high place, in several respects, among the nations of the earth, it is readily admitted that wide-spread evils exist among them, calling loudly for reform. Some of them, like the Poet Laureate, are inclined almost to take a pessimistic view of the state of things.

Tennyson, when a young man, wrote in *Locksley Hall*.—

"Yet I doubt not through the ages an increasing purpose runs,
And the thoughts of men are widened with the process of the suns."

Recent cases of Irish savagery and other things made *Locksley Hall Sixty Years After* adopt a different tone:—

"Gone the cry of 'Forward, Forward,' lost within a growing gloom:
Lost, or only heard in silence from the silence of a tomb.
Half the marvels of my morning, triumphs over time and space,
Staled by frequence, shrunk by usage into commonest commonplace.
'Forward' rang the voices then, and of the many mine was one.
Let us hush this cry of 'Forward' till ten thousand years have gone."

When Englishmen seek to strengthen the hands of Hindu reformers, it is no answer for the orthodox or their allies among "Young India," to point to evils in Britain. Neither are Hindus urged to copy any example because it is English. Some of their customs are neither right nor wrong in themselves, in some they excel the English; only those which are injurious and unjust ought to be abandoned.

Encouragements.—The earlier utterances of Tennyson more nearly express the truth than his later. The cry of "Forward" is not yet "gone," though the progress may be slow. When Rammohun Roy, seventy years ago, began his crusade against widowburning, it found as enthusiastic defenders in Calcutta as early marriages at present The *Dharma Sabha* was founded to preserve this Hindu "institution." The Bengali *Chandrika* was its warm supporter. It was not till 1831, when Rammohun Roy was in England, that the "last appeal of the members of the Dharma Sabha against the abolition of the burning of widows was heard in the Privy Council and rejected."*

As a reformer, Rammohun Roy had to endure much personal obloquy. He writes "I was at last deserted by every person except two or three Scotch friends, to whom and the nation to which they belong, I always feel grateful."†

It must be confessed that the roasting alive of widows would probably still find some defenders in Bengal. Sir Lepel Griffin says, "I was yesterday reading a Bengali newspaper which observed that if the native press had been as strong formerly as at present, the Government would have been unable to abolish suttee."‡

Still, the honour lately done to the memory of Rammohun Roy in Calcutta is a proof of progress.

Another encouraging sign is that the reformers represent the real intellect and knowledge of the country. Mr. Manomohun Ghose expressed the following opinion of "the much-vaunted civilization of India" —

"It must be admitted by all who had carefully studied the ancient literature of India, that the much-vaunted civilization of India was of a peculiar type, and that it never could bear any comparison to what we call modern European civilization. Whatever might have been the case in ancient times, he thought that this frequent appeal to our ancient civilization could serve no good purpose at the present day, while it was simply calculated to make the Bengalis more conceited than they were"

Dr. Bhandarkar, of the Deccan College, a distinguished orientalist, lately expressed the same sentiments in Bombay.

---

* Max Muller's *Biographical Essays*, pp. 25, 26

† Ibid, p. 48

‡ *Asiatic Quarterly Review*, Vol. I p. 475

Really intelligent men among the Hindus, admit the need of reform. The Hon K. T Telang said in Bombay.—

"He thought it well that they should be reminded of their individual or national defects, either by outsiders or by men of their own community, and he was sorry to see the impatience manifested in some quarters at such defects being pointed out. The consciousness of defects was a healthy sign of the first condition of progress, and was not at all incompatible with a proper amount of self-respect"

It is a maxim of national self-conceit and false history that "Reform must come from within." On the contrary, as a rule, "Reform must begin from without." So much is this the case that Sir H. S. Maine, in a Calcutta Convocation Address, traced the root of all progress to the Greeks:—

"With one single exception, no race or nationality, left entirely to itself, has developed any intellectual result which is valuable or durable, except perhaps poetry Not one of all those intellectual achievements which we regard as characteristic of the great progressive races of the world, not the law of the Romans, not the philosophy and sagacity of the Germans, not the luminous order of the French, not the political aptitude of the English—would ever have come into existence, if those races had been left to themselves. To one small people, covering, in its original seat, no more than a hand's breadth of territory, it was given to create the principle of progress, of movement onwards and not backwards or downwards, of destruction tending to construction. That people was the Greek. Except the blind forces of Nature, nothing moves in this world which is not Greek in its origin A ferment spreading from that source has vitalized all the great progressive races of mankind, penetrating from one to another and producing, in each, results accordant with its hidden and latent genius, and results of course often far greater than any exhibited in Greece itself It is this principle of progress which we English are communicating to India. We did not create it We deserve no special credit for it It came to us filtered through many different *media*. But we have received it, and, as we have received it, so we pass it on"

While Greek influence is exaggerated, the general principle is true. Any reform movement, to be thorough, must be taken up in the country, but the original impulse generally comes from without.

Notwithstanding temporary discouragements, the conclusion of the Hon. Mr. Telang may be adopted:—

"He asked them to take a cheerful view of things. Clouds would, of course, sometimes darken the horizon, but they might be sure that these clouds would pass away, and the sun of glory come out again in all its brightness

Need of Leaders.—The ultimate downfall of the caste system is certain in the end. "Truth conquers" Still, it may be much hastened by the efforts of a few zealous, consistent reformers among the higher castes. Mr. Sherring says, "If the superior castes are wise as well as politic, they will lose no time in holding out the right hand of fellowship to the lower. Such a step would, by its magnanimity, secure to them much of the respect and honour which they at present enjoy."

But *deeds* are wanted—not mere *words*.

The Rev. Dr. Miller, of Madras, gave an excellent address on "Nothing for Nothing." Good of any kind is not to be obtained unless men are willing to pay the price for it. Among other things he said that "educated Hindus should not forget that fine discussions and elegant speeches, and long orating would not help them a bit towards removing the great evils of enforced widowhood and infant marriage. There must be action and self-denial." The same remark applies to caste.

It has been suggested that the first step in practical reform would be for different sections of the same caste to eat together and intermarry. Mr. Sherring thinks that such is the case, even at present, to a large extent, among the Rajputs The second advance would be similar intercourse between families of different castes, but of about the same social standing.

A lecture by the Rev. E. P. Rice, B.A., on the "Duties of Citizens," points out an easier way of helping to free one's country from the tyranny of social custom. He says.—

"I am not satisfied with it, but I offer it simply on the principle that half a loaf is better than no bread. If all have not the active aggressive courage required for such a course as I have already named, all may at least muster the passive courage of what is called 'masterly inactivity.' If one is not willing to be made a martyr of, much may be done by standing aloof from the martyrdom of others Refuse to join in the social ostracism by which a heterodox brother is being forced against his conscience, and decline to make any difference in your relations towards him. Probably even this will entail some trouble, but it will be of a minor degree, which ought not to be grudged or to be difficult to bear. It is not necessary that you should agree with the obnoxious member in his opinions or sympathize with his personal character. Of greater importance, it is to side with him in his affirmation of the right of individual liberty. God has made us our brother's helpers, but not our brother's judges Our own need of forbearance from others should make us very forbearing to them. If others choose to persecute, that is their business, but at least we may refuse to have any thing to do with it, and we shall find many of our fellow-countrymen strengthened by our example "*

Duty of the so-called "Lower Castes."—The prospects of caste also depend a good deal upon the course taken by this large section of the community Education is levelling up, and it will have this

* *The Hindu*, 5th August, 1887.

effect more and more Already in Bengal the Vaidyas and the Kayasths occupy a position little inferior to the Brahmans. There are thousands of youths considered to belong to degraded classes now in Colleges and Schools. "The heavy gloom of conscious inferiority," says Sherring, "is passing from their faces, which are becoming bright and cheerful like those of youths of the higher castes."

The lower castes should avail themselves of every opportunity of acquiring knowledge and improving their position. With regard to cleanliness and good manners, they should seek to be on an equality with the highest—to be perfect *gentlemen* in the truest sense of the world. They should also remember that the less airs they give themselves, the more honour they will receive There is a South Indian proverb that "When the low caste is exalted, the umbrella must borne even at midnight." Let the truth of this be disproved

Some of the attempts of the lower castes to raise themselves only damage their cause Dr. Cornish remarks it as a curious phase, "That the lower the caste, the more it now claims pre-eminence for itself" He adds —

'As the lower castes, in those days, frequently send out into the world men who accumulate wealth, so it happens that the surplus funds of such men are often employed in the feeding of pundits to prove the ancient glories of their particular caste. A whole literature of ponderous tomes is springing up in Southern India with no other object than the exaltation of caste."

"The uneasiness of the lower castes in regard to the social position assigned them by Brahmanical authority is simply an indication that, under British rule, they have increased in wealth and intelligence, and naturally desire to prove that the yoke imposed upon them by the caste system was tyrannical and unjust. They seek to accomplish the latter, not by boldly denying the authorities on which the institution of caste was built up, but by claiming a position under the Hindu system which they have no pretensions to"

Referring to the publications on caste, Dr. Cornish says :—

"The majority of the works of this kind are simply mischievous, inasmuch as they encourage, by fanciful theories, the pretensions of humble communities to seek high places in the Hindu social economy, instead of boldly endeavoring to prove historically that the caste system was of foreign growth, imposed upon them by their northern neighbours as a mark of bondage, and consequently no longer applicable to the existing conditions of a free people under an impartial and just Government."*

Fictitious claims only degrade those who make them. The pre-

* *Madras Census Report*, for 1871, pp. 118, 119

tensions of certain castes to be Rajputs are just as false as those of certain Rajputs to be descended from the sun and moon.

A stand should be made on the great principles of truth and justice. Honest useful labour, of whatever kind, as a means of living, is far more honourable than one gained by fraud. The son of a barber who raised himself to be Lord Chancellor of England was only the more deserving of respect on that account.

Religious Reformation the greater Agency—While the measures already mentioned will have some influence, it must be confessed that a religious change is the only effectual remedy. Much was, at one time, expected from education. Mr. Sherring goes so far as to say that, with some noble exceptions, those who have had its advantages are "of all classes the most disappointing" "With all their weight of learning the possession of which enables them to carry of University degrees and honors, they are perfectly content to mingle among the most superstitious and ignorant Hindus, to do as they do, to obey their foolish *dictum* as law, and to have no other aim in life than to conform to the most rigid usages of their ancestors" The testimony of Mr. H. J. S. Cotton, an unexceptionable witness, is much in the same terms:—

"Caste still exercises a predominant influence among all classes of the community. Educated Hindus are puzzled to make out what they owe to their society, and why they render to caste their tribute of submission when there is nothing to compel their obedience Nevertheless, the institution is as powerful among those who disregard many of its rules as it was with their fathers who rigidly observed them all. They find it as hard to bear excommunication themselves, and are as disposed to inflict that punishment upon wrong-doers of their community, as was the case with their ancestors in the past. They find it as desirable to cling to their caste-fellows, despite many disagreeable features in their life and character, as their predecessors may have done."*

Some of them, it is true, make fine speeches. A native newspaper thus compares their public and private life: "A Demosthenes at Debating Societies, whose words tell as peals of thunder, a Luther in his public protestations against prevailing corruption, a thorough-going Cockney in ideas and tastes, he is but a timid crouching Hindu in his home, yielding unquestioning submission to the requisitions of a superstitious family."

Mr. Sherring says of some of the educated classes: "To be satisfied with calmly looking on and watching the current of events, implies a condition of meanness on the one hand, and incapacity, on the other, and therefore of total unfitness to be ranked a whit higher in the scale of civilization than their uneducated, superstitious, and caste-loving neighbours." Even stronger language

* *New India*, p. 142

may be used, for the ignorant have not had their advantages, and are not guilty of insincerity Still worse is the conduct of those described by Principal Wordsworth, whose learning is employed to "vindicate superstition and tyranny."

It is gladly admitted that some of the noblest men in India are also to be found among the educated classes, but they are such a very small minority, that Principal Wordsworth singled out "the learned and venerable Dewan of Indore" as "fighting almost single-handed."

The late Professor of Sanskrit in the Presidency College, Calcutta, in his *Tagore Law Lectures,* describes caste as "the chief characteristic of Hinduism" (p. 44). Caste and Hinduism must fall together. Whatever may be the evils of caste, the masses believe that it has religious sanction, and must be observed at all cost. The Hon. M. G. Ranade said in a letter to Mr. M. Malabari, "Only a religious revival can furnish sufficient moral strength to work out to the complex social problems which demand our attention." The late Keshab Chunder Sen said at Bombay in 1868 "Were I engaged in the work of reforming this country, I would not be busy in lopping off the branches, but I would strike at the fatal root of the tree of corruption, namely—Idolatry. Ninety-nine evils out of every hundred in Hindu society, are, in my opinion, attributable to idolatry and superstition." To these testimonies may be added that of Dr. Duff :—

"What, then, can exorcise this Demon Spirit of caste? Nothing—nothing—but the mighty power of the Spirit of God, quickening, renewing and sanctifying the whole Hindu soul! It is grace, and not argument—regeneration of nature, and not any improved policy of Government—in a word, the gospel, the everlasting gospel, and that alone, savingly brought home by the energy of Jehovah's Spirit, that can *effectually root out and destroy* the gigantic evil. And it is the same energy, inworking through the same gospel of grace and salvation, that can and will root out and destroy the other monster evil under which India still groans—IDOLATRY, with its grim satellite Superstition.

"As *caste* and *idolatry* sprang up together from the same rank soil of old nature—growing with each other's growth, and strengthening with each other's strength—luxuriating in mutual embrace and mysterious wedlock for untold ages—flinging abroad their arms, 'branching so broad and long' as to smite the whole land with the blight of their portentous shadow—both are destined to fall together The same cause will inevitably prove the ruin of both. The same light of sound knowledge, human and divine, accompanied by the grace of God's Spirit, will expose the utter folly and irrationality of idolatry and superstition, and, at one and the same time, lay bare the cruelty and injustice of that strange, half-natural, half-artificial caste system which has done so much to uphold them. Then will the stupendous fabric of idolatry be seen falling down like Dagon before the Ark of the living God; while the antisocial tyrannous dominion of caste will be resented, abhorred, and trampled under foot with an indignation not lessened by the reflection that, over ages and generations without number, it hath already swayed undisturbed the sceptre of a ruthless despotism, which ground men down to the condition of irrationals, and strove to keep them there with the rigour of a merciless necessity."*

A religion whose "chief characteristic" is based on a blasphemous falsehood, will not always retain its hold. It will be seen to be the invention of priestcraft, and its books will no longer be considered as divine. The true Kalki Avatar will yet come, bringing in a reign of righteousness. He will loose the bands of wickedness, undo the heavy burdens, let the oppressed go free, and break every yoke.

The writer would conclude his remarks with Milton's noble prayer:—

"Come forth, from Thy royal chambers, O Prince of all the kings of the earth; put on the visible robes of Thy imperial majesty; take up that unlimited sceptre which Thy Almighty Father hath bequeathed Thee; for now the voice of Thy bride calls Thee, and all creatures sigh to be renewed!"

---

* *The Indian Rebellion*, pp. 357, 358.

ENGLISH PUBLICATIONS

FOR

INDIAN READERS.

PAPERS ON INDIAN REFORM.

This is a Series of Papers treating of the great questions connected with Indian progress—material and moral.

SOCIAL REFORM.

ON DECISION OF CHARACTER AND MORAL COURAGE. 8vo. 56 pp 1½ As. Post-free, 2 As.

A reprint of Foster's celebrated Essay, with some remarks on its application to India.

SANITARY REFORM IN INDIA. 55 pp. 2 As. Post-free, 2½ As

How lakhs of Lives may be saved every year, and crores of cases of Sickness prevented; Precautions against Fever, Cholera, Diabetes, &c.

IS INDIA BECOMING POORER OR RICHER? WITH REMEDIES FOR THE EXISTING POVERTY 8vo. 82 pp. 2½ As. Post-free, 3 As.

The prevailing idea with regard to the increasing poverty of India shown to be incorrect, and the true means of promoting its wealth explained.

DEBT AND THE RIGHT USE OF MONEY. 8vo. 32 pp 1 Anna

Prevalence of Debt in India; its Causes; Evils; how to get out of it; with Franklin's Way to Wealth, &c.

PURITY REFORM. 8vo. 32 pp. 1 Anna

The great need of this reform shown, and the means for its promotion.

TEMPERANCE REFORM IN INDIA. 8vo. 40 pp 1½ As Post-free, 2 As.

CASTE. 8vo. 72 pp. 2 As. Post-free, 2½ As

THE WOMEN OF INDIA AND WHAT CAN BE DONE FOR THEM. 8vo. 158 pp. 4 As Post-free, 5½ As.

THE ABOVE COMPLETE IN ONE VOLUME, 1 Rupee Net. Postage, 2½ As.

PRIZE ESSAY ON THE PROMOTION OF INDIAN DOMESTIC REFORM 8vo 144 pp. 4 As. Post-free, 5 As.

RELIGIOUS REFORM.

POPULAR HINDUISM. 8vo. 96 pp 2½ As Post-free, 3½ As.

Review of the Hinduism of the Epic Poems and Puranas, &c , Rites and Observances; Effects of Hinduism, and Suggested Reforms.

PHILOSOPHIC HINDUISM. 8vo. 72 pp. 2½ As. Post-free, 3 As.

The Upanishads, the Six Schools of Hindu Philosophy, the Minor Schools; Doctrines of Philosophic Hinduism, the Bhagavad Gita; Causes of the Failure of Hindu Philosophy, &c

THE BRAHMA SAMAJ AND OTHER MODERN ECLECTIC RELIGIOUS SYSTEMS. 108 pp 3 As. Post-free, 4 As.

Modern Hindu Theism; Rammohun Roy; Debendranath Tagore; Keshub Chunder Sen, the Sadharan Brahmo Samaj; Madras Brahmoism; Prarthana Samajes.

INDIA HINDU, AND INDIA CHRISTIAN; OR, WHAT HINDUISM HAS DONE FOR INDIA, AND WHAT CHRISTIANITY WOULD DO FOR IT. 8vo. 72 pp. 2½ As. Post-free, 3 As.

Address to thoughtful Hindus, showing how much their country would benefit from the religion which many of them now oppose

KRISHNA AS DESCRIBED IN THE PURANAS AND BHAGAVAD GITA. 8vo. 72 pp 2½ As Post-free, 3 As.

A full account is given of the Krishna Avatara, chiefly taken from the Vishnu Purana, with some extracts from the Bhagavata Purana and the Mahabharata; the circumstances which led to the great war between the Pandus and Kurus are described, and some of the doctrines of the Bhagavad Gita are examined in detail.

ACCOUNT OF THE TEMPLE OF JAGANNATH AT PURI. 8vo. 48 pp. 1½ As

The account is taken chiefly from Dr Rajendralala Mitra's *Antiquities of Orissa*, Hunter's *Gazetteer of India*, Sterling's *Orissa*, &c. With views of the temple, processions and images

CHRISTIANITY EXPLAINED TO A HINDU; OR, THE DOCTRINES OF CHRISTIANITY AND HINDUISM COMPARED 60 pp. 2 As.

Doctrines about God, Creation, the Soul, Karma, Transmigration, Sin, Incarnations, Salvation, Prospects at Death, and Comparative Effects

SWAMI VIVEKANANDA ON HINDUISM 8vo 96 pp. 3 As. Post-free, 4 As.

The Swami's Chicago Address is quoted in full and examined, important facts are brought out which he omitted to state

THE HISTORY OF CHRISTIANITY IN INDIA; WITH ITS PROSPECTS. 8vo. 150 pp. 5 As. Post-free, 6 As.

An account of the early Christian Missions, and the progress of Christianity among the principal nations, with 35 illustrations, including portraits of some eminent Missionaries.

TESTIMONIES OF GREAT MEN TO THE BIBLE AND CHRISTIANITY. 8vo. 45 pp 1½ As. Post-free, 2 As

Opinions expressed by great writers, philosophers, scientists, lawyers and statesmen, showing that the Bible and Christianity are firmly believed by the most eminent men of the time.

HOW THE PEOPLE OF ANCIENT EUROPE BECAME CHRISTIANS, AND THE FUTURE RELIGION OF INDIA. 8vo. 48 pp. 1½ As Post-free, 2 As.

CIVILIZATION, ANCIENT AND MODERN, COMPARED; WITH REMARKS ON THE STUDY OF SANSKRIT. 8vo. 48 pp. 1½ As. Post-free, 2 As.

DEVIL-DANCERS, WITCH-FINDERS, RAIN-MAKERS, AND MEDICINE MEN. 4to. 60 pp 2½ As. Post-free, 3 As.

A full account of these curious and degrading superstitions, prevalent among backward nations in different parts of the world, with 36 illustrations.

TRACTS FOR MUHAMMADANS. 12mo. 120 pp. 3 As.

By the Rev Dr. G Rouse, M. A Translated from the Bengali The Integrity of the Gospel; Jesus or Muhammad?; The Sinless Prophet; The True Islam; The Koran, Fatiha, The Paraclete, &c., are some of the subjects.

DODDRIDGE'S RISE AND PROGRESS OF RELIGION IN THE SOUL. 12mo. 180 pp. 3 As. Post-free, 4 As.

Pice Papers on Indian, Reform ¼ Anna each.

Some are original, others are abridged from the foregoing for popular use

1. Causes of Indian Poverty
2. Indian Marriage Customs
3 Supposed and Real Causes of Disease.
4. Patriotism. False and True
5. Management of Infants.
6. Debt, and How to Get Out of it.
7. The Purdah; or the Seclusion of Indian Women.
8. Caste: its Origin and Effects.
9 Astrology.
10 What has the British Government done for India?
11. Who wrote the Vedas?
12. Manava-Dharma Sastra.
13 The Bhagavad Gita.
14 The Science of the Hindu Sastras.
15. Fevers: their Causes, Treatment, and Prevention.
16 Cholera and Bowel Complaints.
17. Animal Worship.
18. Early Marriage, its Evils and Suggested Reforms.
19. Duty to a Wife
20. The Fruits of Hinduism.
21. Indian Widows and what should be done for them.
22. The Advantages of female education.
23 Hindu and Christian Worship Compared.
24 Hindu Pilgrimages.
25. Charity: False and True.
26. The Two Watchwords—Custom and Progress.
27. The Value of Pure Water.
28. Charms, Mantras and other Superstitions.
29. Nautches.
30. Importance of Cleanliness.
31. How to have Healthy Children
32. How to bring up Children
33. How to take Care of the Sick.
34. Eclipses.
35. Family Prayer.
36. Giving Abuse.
37. Shraddhas.
38. Karma or Fate.
39. The Fatherhood of God.
40. The Brotherhood of Man.
41. Hindu and Christian Ideals of Piety.
42. Prayaschitta.

Complete in a volume half bound gilt title, 1 Re. Postage, 2 As.

Descriptions of Countries and Peoples.

PICTORIAL TOUR ROUND INDIA. Imperial 8vo. 116 pp. 6 As. Post-free, 7½ As.

An imaginary tour round India, with visits to Nepal and Cashmere, describing the principal cities and other objects of interest. With 97 woodcuts illustrative of the Himalayas, Calcutta, Benares, Agra, Delhi, Bombay, Madras, &c.

THE PRINCIPAL NATIONS OF INDIA. 8vo. 160 pp. 4 As. Post-free, 5 As.

An account of 42 Nations and Tribes of India, with specimens of some of their languages, and 55 illustrations.

THE NATIVE STATES OF INDIA AND THEIR PRINCES; WITH NOTICES OF SOME IMPORTANT ZEMINDARIS. 4to. 100 pp. 5 As. Post-free, 6 As.

157 States are described, and 32 portraits are given. The little book will help to enable Indians to understand the vast extent of their country, and what is being done for its improvement.

KASI, OR BENARES, the Holy City of the Hindus. Imperial 8vo. 44 pp. 3 As. Post-free, 4 As.

An account of the city; its Sanskrit schools, ghats, temples, and pilgrimages; with 23 illustrations.

THE GREAT TEMPLES OF INDIA, CEYLON AND BURMA. Imperial 8vo. 104 pp. with 60 illustrations. 6 As. Post-free, 7½ As.

There are pictures and descriptions of some of the most celebrated Hindu, Sikh, Jain, and Buddhist temples; as Puri, Budh-Gaya, Benares, Hurdwar, Gangotri, Ellora, Elephanta, Amritsar, Gwalior, Tanjore, Srirangam, Kandy, Prome, and Mandalay.

BURMA AND THE BURMESE. 4to. 54 pp. 2½ As. Post-free, 3 As.

A description of the manners and customs of the Burmese; an account of their government, religion, and history, with illustrative woodcuts, and portraits of King Theebaw and his Queen.

LANKA AND ITS PEOPLE; OR A DESCRIPTION OF CEYLON. 4to. 72 pp. 3 As. Post-free, 3½ As.

The account of Lanka given in the Ramayana is first mentioned. Its history and present condition are then described, with numerous illustrative woodcuts.

TIBET: THE HIGHEST COUNTRY IN THE WORLD. 4to. 64 pp. 2½ As.

An account of the country, its productions, the curious customs of the people, their religions and supposed living incarnations; with numerous illustrations.

PICTORIAL TOUR ROUND ENGLAND, SCOTLAND, AND IRELAND. Imperial 8vo. 114 pp. 6 As. Post-free, 7½ As.

Descriptions of the chief places of interest; Public Schools and Universities; Coal Mines and Manufactures; the British Government; Home Life; England an example and warning to India. With 104 woodcuts, and coloured engraving of the Queen-Empress.

PICTURES OF CHINA AND ITS PEOPLE. 4to. 56 pp. 2½ As. Post-free, 3 As.

Extent, History; Manners and Customs of the People; Schools, Examinations; Industries; Travelling; Language and Literature; Government; Religions; India and China compared; with 64 Illustrations.

JAPAN: THE LAND OF THE RISING SUN. 4to. 68 pp. 2½ As. Post-free, 3 As.

With 49 Illustrations. An interesting description of this beautiful country, and an account of the remarkable changes which have taken place in it.

PICTORIAL TOUR ROUND BIBLE LANDS. Imperial 8vo. 100 pp 6 As. Post-free, 7½ As

The principal countries mentioned in the Bible and in ancient history are described, as Palestine, Syria, Bombay, Asia Minor, Greece and Italy, with 104 Illustrations

ARABIA, AND ITS PROPHET. 4to 64 pp 2½ As Post-free, 3 As.

An account of the Arabs; with descriptions of Jeddah, Mecca, Medina, the History of Muhammad and the early Caliphs, the Koran, Muslim Doctrines, Sects, Prayers, Pilgrimage, &c., with numerous illustrations

PICTURES OF RUSSIA AND ITS PEOPLES. Imperial 8vo 83 pp. 5 As

A description both of European and Asiatic Russia, including an account of the different races by which they are peopled, their manners and customs, the Government, &c; with 89 illustrations and maps

PICTURES OF WOMEN IN MANY LANDS. Imperial 8vo. 112 pp. 6 As Post-free, 7½ As

Descriptions of women, beginning with the most degraded nations of the world, and gradually ascending to the most enlightened, with suggestions, from the review, for Indian women, with 172 illustrations

---

Biographies.

STATESMEN OF RECENT TIMES. 8vo. 192 pp. 8 As. Post-free, 9½ As.

Accounts are given of the leading Statesmen in the great countries of the world, as Gladstone, Salisbury, Bismarck and others. Special notice is taken of those interested in India. In all 182 are mentioned, with 122 portraits

THE GOVERNORS-GENERAL OF INDIA, First Series. By Henry Morris, M. C. S. (Retired. 8vo. 145 pp. 4 As. Post-free, 5 As.

Contains sketches of the lives of Warren Hastings, Lord Cornwallis, Sir John Shore, Marquis Wellesley, the Earl of Minto, and the Marquis of Hastings, with portraits Interesting personal details are given, such as are not usually found in histories

THE GOVERNORS-GENERAL OF INDIA, Second Series. By the same author, 8vo. 175 pp. 4 As. Post-free, 5 As.

Including Sketches of Lord Amherst, Lord William Bentinck, Lord Auckland, Lord Ellenborough, Lord Hardinge, and the Marquis of Dalhousie.

The two Series, half bound in cloth, gilt title, 12 As.

SKETCHES OF INDIAN CHRISTIANS; WITH AN INTRODUCTION BY S SATTHIANADAN, M.A. 8vo. 268 pp half cloth gilt title, 10 As. Post-free, 11½ As.

An account of 42 Indian Protestant Christians; Tamil, Telugu, Canarese, Malayalam, Bengali, Hindustani, Panjabi, Afghan, Gujarati, Marathi, Parsi, and Karen, with several portraits

ANGLO-INDIAN WORTHIES: By Henry Morris, MADRAS C.S (Retired.) 8vo. 160 pp. 4 As. Post-free, 5 As. Full cloth, gilt title, 8 As.

Lives of Sir Thomas Munro, Sir John Malcolm, Lord Metcalfe, Mountstuart Elphinstone, James Thomason, Sir Henry Lawrence, Sir James Outram, Sir Donald Macleod, and Sir Bartle Frere, with portraits.

EMINENT FRIENDS OF MAN; or LIVES OF DISTINGUISHED PHILANTHROPISTS. 8vo. 158 pp. 4 As. Post-free, 5 As. Full cloth, gilt title, 10 As.

Sketches of Howard, Oberlin, Granville Sharp, Clarkson, Wilberforce, Buxton, Pounds, Davies of Devanden, George Moore, Montefiore, Livesey, the Earl of Shaftesbury, and others; with remarks on what might be done in India.

SOME NOTED INDIANS OF MODERN TIMES. 8vo. 164 pp. 4 As Post-free, 5 As.

Sketches of Indian Religious and Social Reformers, Philanthropists, Scholars, Statesmen, Judges, Journalists, and others, with several portraits.

MARTIN LUTHER, THE GREAT EUROPEAN REFORMER. 8vo. 100 pp. 2½ As. Post-free, 3 As.

The state of religion in Europe in the time of Luther is described; a full account is given of his undaunted efforts to bring about a reformation, the greater need of a similar change in India is shown, and Luther is held up as an example. 15 illustrations.

BABA PADMANJI. An Autobiography. 8vo. 108 pp. 2½ As. Post-free, 3 As.

An interesting account by himself of this popular Marathi author, describing his conversion from Hinduism to Christianity.

PICTURE STORIES OF NOBLE WOMEN. 4to. 50 pp. 2½ As. Post-free, 3 As.

Account of Cornelia, Agrippina, Padmani of Chittore, Lady Jane Grey, Ahaliya Bai, Mrs. Fry, Princess Alice, Miss Carpenter, Maharani Surnomayi, Pandita Ramabai, Miss Nightingale, and Lady Dufferin.

THE QUEEN-EMPRESS OF INDIA AND HER FAMILY. 43 pp. 3 As. Post-free, 3½ As.

Her early life; marriage; widowhood; children; progress in India during her reign; traits of character and lessons from her life. With 27 illustrations, and a coloured portrait of the Empress.

SIR HERBERT EDWARDES. By Henry Morris. 8vo 20 pp. ½ Anna.

Publications for Students.

SELECT CONVOCATION ADDRESSES, delivered to Graduates of the Madras University. 8vo. 231 pp. Stiff covers, 8 As.; Half bound in cloth, 12 As. Full bound in cloth, with gilt title, 1 Re. Post-free.

The volume contains 15 addresses, commencing in 1859, and including several of the most recent. Some of the most distinguished men in South India during the last 30 years took part in the Series. Many very useful hints to young men entering upon the battle of life in any part of India will be found in the collection.

THE INDIAN STUDENT'S MANUAL 12mo. 352 pp. 8 As. Post-free, 9 As.

Hints on Studies, Examinations, Moral Conduct, Religious Duties, and Success in Life.

Progress.

This is a monthly illustrated Periodical for the educated classes in India and Ceylon. The subscription is only 8 As. a year; with postage, 14 As. Three copies may be sent for ½ anna postage.

Orders to be addressed to Mr. A. T. SCOTT, Tract Depôt, MADRAS.

Printed at the M. E. Publishing House, Mount Road, Madras—1896.

CPSIA information can be obtained at www.ICGtesting.com
Printed in the USA
LVOW03s0311240815

451274LV00015B/199/P